BRITISH
WARSHIPS
&

G000112050

HMS Dragon

THE ROYAL NAVY

Speaking to an audience, in July 2014, at the Navy league's International Leadership Breakfast, the First Sea Lord, Admiral Sir George Zambellas, said the christening of the aircraft carrier QUEEN ELIZABETH is part of a 'maritime renaissance' for the RN and represents 'part of a second great Elizabethan era.' I am sure he is right. In recent years billions have been spent on new ships. The elderly Type 42 destroyers have now been replaced by the Type 45; the small Invincible class carriers have been decommissioned, shortly to be replaced by the large Queen Elizabeth-class; the nuclear-powered submarine fleet is witnessing the introduction of the Astute-class to replace the Swiftsure and Trafalgar-class boats, while work continues to design a replacement for the Vanguard-class Trident missile submarines. The Type 23 frigates are to be replaced by the Type 26 and there are Offshore Patrol Vessels and tankers under construction. To the casual observer this could certainly be perceived as a 'maritime renaissance', however, it should more accurately be seen as a phoenix rising from the ashes of a Royal Navy slashed to the bone by repeated defence cuts - stripped of ships, submarines, aircraft and personnel, while at the same time facing ever more demands on its resources. 2015 is going to be a defining year for UK Defence - a general election and the second Strategic Defence and Security Review. Already the wording and posturing with regard to matters of defence are ringing alarm bells - there remains talk of more cuts to come. Where the axe will fall will not become clear until after the election, but fall, it will, and with it will come more pain for the Royal Navy and more harsh decisions with regards to what to give up.

On a daily basis, the Royal Navy has ships deployed on three concurrent tasks - Operation Kipion; Atlantic Patrol Tasking (North) and Atlantic Patrol Tasking (South). Operation Kipion is the over-arching task for those vessels deployed on operations across the Gulf, Red Sea and Indian Ocean, supporting maritime security operations and anti-piracy as required. The operation is supported by the 9th MCMS based at Bahrain (ATHERSTONE, CHIDDINGFOLD, PENZANCE and SHOREHAM) supported by RFA CARDIGAN BAY. There is a roulement element comprising two escorts with one usually in the Red Sea and the other in the Gulf - these vessels used to rotate from the UK on deployments of up to seven months. In 2014, it was announced that these operations would be extended to nine months.

The Atlantic Patrol Task (North) provides a presence in the Caribbean and the North Atlantic to act as a deterrent to drug smugglers and to provide humanitarian cover during the hurricane season. In recent years, this commitment has been provided by either a Royal Navy destroyer or frigate, or an RFA vessel with embarked air support.

The Atlantic Patrol Task (South), traditionally provided an escort for operations around the Falkland Islands and South Georgia, providing ongoing protection and reassurance to British interests. However, in recent years the Offshore Patrol Vessel CLYDE has become the de facto Falklands Islands guard ship and the destroyer or frigate on task has taken on a much more diverse role. Its operating area has extend from the Falkands in the south to the eastern seaboard of South America across to the west coast of Africa - millions of square miles of ocean covered by a single warship.

To cover these three tasks - providing four warships on station, requires a roulement of twelve ships - that is three for each task. One on station; one transiting to or from station and a third in maintenance having returned or working up preparing to deploy. Today, the Royal Navy only has nineteen ships from which these twelve can come. This leaves just seven ships available (of which up to three may be in refit at any one time) to cover all other contingencies - be that defence of UK waters; response to world events - humanitarian or military; or training and exercises necessary to maintain crew and equipment at a high level of readiness for their primary role of escorting the high value Royal Navy units and task groups.

One such task group is the Response Force Task Group (RFTG), the Royal Navy's expeditionary task force formed as part of the SDSR 10 move towards highly mobile expeditionary warfare capabilities. The RFTG is maintained at high-readiness to respond to global events. While its priority is centred around amphibious warfare operations, the RFTG is capable of undertaking a wide range of activities such as evacuation, disaster relief or humanitarian operations. It has deployed every year since 2010 under the Cougar banner, usually with much fanfare. Exercise Cougar 2014 was a much more subdued affair. There was very little pre-deployment press information and when the group deployed in early September, it comprised BULWARK, OCEAN, LYME BAY and WAVE KNIGHT - not a single escort. After a few initial exercises in the Mediterranean the RFTG was joined by the German frigate SCHLESWIG-HOLSTEIN, prior to deploying east of Suez. Once in the Red Sea, the RFTG comprised BULWARK, LYME BAY, SCHLESWIG-HOLSTEIN, and units deployed on Operation Kipion - OCEAN and WAVE KNIGHT had detached in the Mediterranean and returned to the UK. I find it strange that a group of ships operating as the RFTG can change its composition so many times during such a short deployment. A task group becomes effective by operating and training as a unit. For it to be effective it must maintain its struc-

3

ture throughout. Stranger still is the apparent lack of a substantial number of helicopters. I have said this before, but, if the RFTG is truly a high-readiness asset surely it should deploy with 100% capability, which would include Royal Marines, their vehicles and equipment and a full Tailored Air Group ready to respond to global events - as a high-readiness unit it cannot be expected to return to the UK to pick up a full complement of vehicles, aircraft or troops if it were required for contingent operations during its deployment - and sailing four high-value ships without an escort is sheer folly. Since inception RFTG has been a paper asset as it seems government is not willing to put up the funding to maintain a true high-readiness capability. Perhaps this, together with the lack of available escorts is why Cougar 14 was so low key.

It is evident that such a small number of escorts cannot sustain the current tempo of operations placed upon them. The fewer ships you have, the harder each has to work. The harder they work, the more maintenance they require. The more maintenance they require, the less time they are available for tasking. In late 2014, the Offshore Patrol Vessel SEVERN, became the first such vessel to deploy on Atlantic Patrol Task (North). She will spend the winter months in the Caribbean conducting counter narcotics operations and providing a UK presence in the area. This is a radical change in operations and is seen as a 'proof of concept' deployment to assess the ability of such vessels to undertake a sustained and unsupported patrol task in the Caribbean. The Royal Navy have not yet determined whether they will operate both the River-class and Batch II River-class ships, FORTH, MEDWAY and TYNE, being built by BAE Systems, or whether the latter will replace the former (such funding issues are for SDSR 15). However, the outcome could be that in future, the Batch II River-class could become the three ship roulement for APT(N), thereby releasing three frontline warships for other operations. It has long been contended that placing a sophisticated escort in the Caribbean for counter narcotics operations, or in the Red Sea for counter-piracy is a waste of a valuable asset. Are we to see these new OPVs taking on more of the policing roles - the start of a two tier RN?

The benefit to the MoD is twofold. Firstly, if these new vessels are deployed on enduring commitments and tasking, there would be an opportunity to decrease the frigate force by three. Three of the four orphan Type 23s not being upgraded could be decommissioned - MoD would cover itself by saying that there are still 19 vessels available for tasking, while at the same time releasing crews, particularly engineers, to fill gaps. The second benefit comes when ordering the Type 26, which the government constantly sell as being a 'like for like' replacement. By the time the first order is placed, 'like for like' will now mean acquiring ten ships thereby instantly saving the cost of three new frigates. Already the government are changing the manner in which they refer to Type 26 orders. Initial talk of 'like for like' replacement of the Type 23 (13 ships) has given way to an 'initial order of eight' and more recently a class of 'up to 13 ships' - something that will be very familiar to those with any memory of the Type 45 destroyer acquisition (a class of 12 was reduced to a class of 'up to 12', then eight and finally just six).

Maybe it will be inevitable that the Royal Navy will lose more ships because, in addition to the strain on the operational planners in assigning ships to operations, there is the question of manpower. For years, even decades, the Royal Navy has massaged its manpower to try to maintain an operational tempo. Most ships have gaps in their crews, but with a little judicious juggling, there has always appeared to be the right numbers on the important deployments when needed. Of late it has become evident that the Royal Navy are nursing a massive manpower crisis with regard to engineering staff (something the RFA is also struggling with). Despite, large financial deals to remain, engineers are leaving the service in high numbers - driven by changing conditions of service within the RN; lack of shore time as billets are filled by civilian contractors; lured by far more lucrative careers in the civilian sector or maybe the fact that 280 engineers were made redundant under SDSR 10. The end result is a huge loss of experienced personnel and ever increasing difficulty in filling billets. So much so that in 2014 the RN and the US Coast Guard signed an agreement whereby US Coast Guard engineering staff would come to the UK for three year stints to help man the Type 23 frigates.

The RN has many challenges to face in the coming years. With decreasing budgets it will have to sustain a huge shipbuilding programme. The Successor submarine programme is expected to cost over £11 billion, just to build the submarines. The new aircraft carriers will continue to eat up large chunks of the budget and with the recent announcement that it is intended to keep both carriers, attention must now switch to acquiring the aircraft to fly from them. The first four production F-35B Lightnings were ordered towards the end of 2014, with further annual batches of four being ordered through 2018. Even more will be needed if the RN is to operate a true naval strike capability and not just field two aircraft carriers unable to contribute to operations. The Type 26 frigate programme will start gearing up in 2016 and again this will be another big ticket item, taking up big chunks of the budget for many years. Regeneration of equipment and capabilities post-Afghanistan and refocussing on operations off Syria, Iraq and Ukraine is going to have an effect on operational tempo. Finally the manpower crisis is going to have to be addressed so that those ships and aircraft which are in service can be operated and deployed when needed.

While speaking at Farnborough in mid-July 2014, the Prime Minister touched upon the forthcoming SDSR. While he recognised that SDSR 10 was brutal, and necessarily so in order to close the black hole of defence overspending, he went on to state that SDSR 2015 "....will be similar to that, but hopefully it won't be quite as challenging as the last SDSR...."

The last SDSR failed on many levels to deliver - far from being a strategic led review, it was driven by budget, and the desire to cut costs. The Royal Navy of 2015 has been reduced to a shadow of its former self. It is operationally stretched and the demands being placed upon equipment and personnel to achieve the strategic aims of government are at their maximum. If SDSR 2015 does introduce further cuts it is difficult to see what can be axed without having an adverse effect on operations. It will be time for the First Sea Lord to go to government and ask what strategic aims he is willing to give up because, put in simple terms, another budget driven review will leave the Royal Navy unable to fulfill the demands placed upon it by government.

The First Sea Lord is right to say that the RN is undergoing a maritime renaissance - and I am sure that he is a very firm hand on the tiller, but so fragile is that recovery, that unless the government commit to continued investment to support its strategic aspirations, the rising phoenix of the Royal Navy will quickly return to the ashes from which it is so desperately trying to emerge.

SHIPS OF THE ROYAL NAVY
Pennant Numbers

Ship	Pennant Number	Page	Ship	Pennant Number	Page
Assault Ships			VIGILANT	S30	9
			VENGEANCE	S31	9
OCEAN	L12	13	TIRELESS	S88	12
ALBION *	L14	14	TORBAY	S90	12
BULWARK	L15	14	TRENCHANT	S91	12
			TALENT	S92	12
Destroyers			TRIUMPH	S93	12
			ASTUTE	S119	10
DARING	D32	15	AMBUSH	S120	10
DAUNTLESS	D33	15			
DIAMOND	D34	15	**Minehunters**		
DRAGON	D35	15			
DEFENDER	D36	15	LEDBURY	M30	19
DUNCAN	D37	15	CATTISTOCK	M31	19
			BROCKLESBY	M33	19
Frigates			MIDDLETON	M34	19
			CHIDDINGFOLD	M37	19
KENT	F78	17	ATHERSTONE	M38	19
PORTLAND	F79	17	HURWORTH	M39	19
SUTHERLAND	F81	17	QUORN	M41	19
SOMERSET	F82	17	PENZANCE	M106	21
ST ALBANS	F83	17	PEMBROKE	M107	21
LANCASTER	F229	17	GRIMSBY	M108	21
ARGYLL	F231	17	BANGOR	M109	21
IRON DUKE	F234	17	RAMSEY	M110	21
MONMOUTH	F235	17	BLYTH	M111	21
MONTROSE	F236	17	SHOREHAM	M112	21
WESTMINSTER	F237	18			
NORTHUMBERLAND	F238	18	**Patrol Craft**		
RICHMOND	F239	18			
			EXPRESS	P163	25
Submarines			EXPLORER	P164	25
			EXAMPLE	P165	25
VANGUARD	S28	9	EXPLOIT	P167	25
VICTORIOUS	S29	9	CLYDE	P257	23

HMS Victorious

SUBMARINES
VANGUARD CLASS

Ship	Pennant Number	Completion Date	Builder
VANGUARD	S28	1992	VSEL
VICTORIOUS	S29	1994	VSEL
VIGILANT	S30	1997	VSEL
VENGEANCE	S31	1999	VSEL

Displacement 15,980 tons (dived) **Dimensions** 149.9m x 12.8m x 12m **Speed** 25 + dived **Armament** 16 Tubes for Trident 2 (D5) missiles, 4 Torpedo Tubes **Complement** 135

Notes

After the first successful UK D5 missile firing in May '94 the first operational patrol was carried out in early '95 and a patrol has been constantly maintained ever since. The UK's Trident missiles have been de-targeted since 1994, and the submarine on deterrent patrol is normally at several days notice to fire her missiles. Due to delays in the Successor submarine programme, the service life of the Vanguard class has been extended to beyond 2028 while at the same time reducing the number of operational missiles on each submarine to just eight. To achieve this five year extension three additional Long Overhaul Periods (LOPs) will be required, at Devonport, costing around £1.3 billion between 2014 and 2024. It is anticipated that VANGUARD will re-enter the refit cycle in 2015.

HMS Astute (with dry deck shelter)

ASTUTE CLASS

Ship	Pennant Number	Completion Date	Builder
ASTUTE	S119	2009	BAe Submarine Solutions
AMBUSH	S120	2012	BAe Submarine Solutions
ARTFUL	S121	2015	BAe Submarine Solutions
AUDACIOUS	S122	2018	BAe Submarine Solutions
ANSON	S123	2020	BAe Submarine Solutions
AGAMEMNON	S124	2022	BAe Submarine Solutions
AJAX	S125	2024	BAe Submarine Solutions

Displacement 7,400 tonnes (7,800 dived) **Dimensions** 97m x 11.2m x 9.5m **Speed** 29+ dived **Armament** 6 Torpedo Tubes; Spearfish torpedoes; Tomahawk cruise missiles for a payload of 38 weapons **Complement** 98 (Accommodation for 12 Officers and 97 Ratings)

Notes

Ordered in 1997, the Astute class will replace the Trafalgar class in RN service. AMBUSH was commissioned on 1 March 2013, having arrived at Faslane on 19 September 2012. The third boat ARTFUL was launched on 19 May 2014 and conducted her first basin dive on 7/8 October. She is scheduled to enter service in 2015. The hull of AUDACIOUS is nearing completion and commissioning work should be underway in 2014. She is the first to benefit from a so-called Design for Cost Reduction initiative, a redesign activity pursued by BAE Systems, the MoD and its key suppliers to ensure the affordability of later boats, addressing both the platform and combat system. As well as re-engineering certain parts of the original design, there was a move to commercial-off-the-shelf systems for some of the combat system equipments.

All major fabrications for ANSON are now complete and awaiting assembly. The keel ring for the sixth submarine, AGAMEMNON, was ceremonially laid down on 18 July 13. The seventh submarine, AJAX, has been confirmed, but not yet ordered.

The Astute class is designed to fulfil a range of key strategic and tactical roles including anti-ship and anti-submarine operations, surveillance and intelligence gathering and support for land forces. Each boat will have a lock in lock out capability, enabling swimmers to leave the submarine while dived. This capability is in addition to the Chalfont dry deck hangar which can be fitted to the aft casing and designed to hold a swimmer delivery vehicle for stand off insertion.

Both ASTUTE and AMBUSH returned to the Clyde in October 2014 on completion of their maiden operational deployments, the former spent eight months in the Mediterranean and east of Suez, while the latter had spent three months off the east coast of the USA and South America.

The planned in-service dates for the remainder of the Astute class boats are: AUDACIOUS (2018); ANSON (2020); AGAMEMNON (2022) and AJAX (2024).

11

TRAFALGAR CLASS

Ship	Pennant Number	Completion Date	Builder
TORBAY	S90	1986	Vickers
TRENCHANT	S91	1989	Vickers
TALENT	S92	1990	Vickers
TRIUMPH	S93	1991	Vickers

Displacement 4,500 tons 5,200 tons dived **Dimensions** 85.4m x 9.8m x 9.5m **Speed** 30+ dived **Armament** 5 Torpedo Tubes; Spearfish torpedoes; Tomahawk cruise missiles for a payload of 24 weapons **Complement** 130

Notes

TORBAY, TALENT, TRENCHANT and TRIUMPH have undergone upgrade and received Type 2076 Sonar. In September 2013 TRENCHANT began a substantial two year Revalidation and Assisted Maintenance Period at Devonport, having returned, in May, from a record breaking 335 day patrol, including 267 days east of Suez. Beginning in 2014 the final four submarines are to undergo a communications package upgrade to overcome obsolescence issues. With delays to the Astute class, decommissioning dates for the remaining T class have been extended. TIRELESS was decommissioned 19 June 2014 leaving just four Trafalgar class submarines in service. As at July 2013 they are scheduled to decommission as follows: TORBAY (2017); TRENCHANT (2019); TALENT (2021) and TRIUMPH (2022).

HMS Ocean

LANDING PLATFORM HELICOPTER OCEAN

Ship	Pennant Number	Completion Date	Builder
OCEAN	L12	1998	Kvaerner

Displacement 22,500 tonnes **Dimensions** 203.8m x 35m x 6.6m **Speed** 17 knots **Armament** 3 x Phalanx, 4 x 30mm ASC guns, 4 x Minigun **Aircraft** Tailored Air Group (Merlin, Sea King, Chinook, Apache as required) **Complement** Ship 285, Squadrons 206 (maximum 1275 including Royal Marines)

Notes

Can carry 12 Sea King and 6 Lynx helicopters. RAF Chinook helicopters are normally carried as an integral part of the ship's air group, but they are unable to be stowed below decks. Vessel is somewhat constrained by her slow speed. Many improvements have been made to her including accommodation for both crew and embarked Royal Marines; advanced communications facilities; a better weapon defence system and an upgrade to the ship's aviation support facilities to improve support to helicopter operations including the Apache attack helicopter. She completed a 15-month refit at Devonport in July 2014. Major upgrades included the installation of Type 997 (Artisan) radar and the replacing of the 20mm guns by four 30mm Automated Small Calibre gun systems. She resumed the LPH role from ILLUSTRIOUS (which decommissioned on 28 August 2014). She sailed in August as part of the Cougar 2014 deployment conducting exercises with Albanian and French forces.

13

HMS Bulwark

LANDING PLATFORM DOCK

ALBION CLASS

Ship	Pennant Number	Completion Date	Builder
ALBION	L14	2003	BAe Systems
BULWARK	L15	2004	BAe Systems

Displacement 18,500 tons, 21,500 tons (flooded) **Dimensions** 176m x 25.6m x 7.1m
Speed 18 knots **Armament** 2 x CIWS, 2 x 20mm guns (single) **Complement** 325
Military Lift 303 troops, with an overload capacity of a further 405

Notes

Vehicle deck capacity for up to six Challenger 2 tanks or around 30 armoured all-terrain tracked vehicles. Floodable well dock able to take four utility landing craft. Four smaller landing craft carried on davits. Two-spot flight deck able to take medium support helicopters and stow a third. Flight deck allows the simultaneous operation of two Chinook helicopters. These vessels do not have a hangar but have equipment needed to support aircraft operations. Only one of the class remains operational at this time. BULWARK assumed the role of fleet flagship in October 2011. In 2012 ALBION entered a 33-month period of extended readiness during which time she provided training for Landing Craft Davit operations. It is anticipated that she will begin a regeneration refit in 2015 and rejoin the fleet in 2016 to replace BULWARK as the operational LPD.

HMS Duncan

DESTROYERS
DARING CLASS
(Type 45)

Ship	Pennant Number	Completion Date	Builder
DARING	D32	2008	BVT Surface Fleet
DAUNTLESS	D33	2008	BVT Surface Fleet
DIAMOND	D34	2009	BVT Surface Fleet
DRAGON	D35	2011	BVT Surface Fleet
DEFENDER	D36	2012	BVT Surface Fleet
DUNCAN	D37	2013	BVT Surface Fleet

Displacement 7,350 tons **Dimensions** 152.4m x 21.2m x 5.7m **Speed** 29 knots **Armament** 1 - 4.5-inch gun, Sea Viper missile system comprising Sylver VLS with combination of up to 48 Aster 15 and Aster 30 missiles, 2 x Vulcan Phalanx (fitted as required) **Aircraft** Lynx or Merlin **Complement** 190 (with space for 235)

Notes

Originally to have been a class of "up to" 12 ships this was reduced to just six. DRAGON was the first of the batch two destroyers, which include upgrades to systems onboard in line with technological developments.

The ships are capable of contributing to worldwide maritime and joint operations in multi threat environments and are primarily air defence ships. The Sea Viper missile ensures that the ships can destroy incoming threats from the air whilst the Sampson Multi-Function Radar can simultaneously detect and track over four hundred targets, providing a fully automatic operation where rapid reaction is required. In 2013 DARING participated in an anti-ballistic missile exercise with the US Navy in the Pacific to prove the Sampson radar in that mode. Although there are no plans to field an ABM missile, 2015 funding has been provided to demonstrate Sampson running ABM and AAW functions simultaneously.

In order to give the ships an anti-ship capability it is intended that the Harpoon missile systems removed from the decommissioned Batch III Type 22 frigates will be fitted to four of the Type 45 destroyers. DUNCAN was noted in 2014 with the deck mounts for Harpoon in place and is expected to be the first to go to sea with the system fitted.

In June 2014 The MoD awarded BAE Systems a £70 million contract to manage the support, maintenance and upgrade of the Type 45 destroyers at Portsmouth Naval Base and on all their operations, both in the UK and globally.

FRIGATES
DUKE CLASS (Type 23)

Ship	Pennant Number	Completion Date	Builder
KENT	F78	2000	Yarrow
PORTLAND	F79	2000	Yarrow
SUTHERLAND	F81	1997	Yarrow
SOMERSET	F82	1996	Yarrow
ST ALBANS	F83	2001	Yarrow
LANCASTER	F229	1991	Yarrow
ARGYLL	F231	1991	Yarrow
IRON DUKE	F234	1992	Yarrow
MONMOUTH	F235	1993	Yarrow
MONTROSE	F236	1993	Yarrow
WESTMINSTER	F237	1993	Swan Hunter
NORTHUMBERLAND	F238	1994	Swan Hunter
RICHMOND	F239	1994	Swan Hunter

Displacement 4,900 tonnes **Dimensions** 133m x 16.1m x 5m **Speed** 28 knots **Armament** Harpoon & Seawolf missile systems: 1 - 4.5-inch gun, 2 - single 30mm guns, 4 - 2 twin, magazine launched, Torpedo Tubes, Lynx or Merlin helicopter **Complement** 185

Notes

Now the sole class of frigate in RN service, the ships incorporate 'Stealth' technology to minimise magnetic, radar, acoustic and infra-red signatures. Gas turbine and diesel electric propulsion. Type 2087 Sonar is to be fitted in only 9 of the remaining 13 of the class (ARGYLL, MONTROSE, MONMOUTH and IRON DUKE will not receive the upgrade). MONTROSE is in refit until 2016.

In August 2008 the MoD announced that the Type 996 surveillance and target indication radar was to be replaced by the ARTISAN 3D Medium Range Radar (now designated Type 997) under a £100 million contract covering demonstration, manufacturing, delivery and the first 10 years of in-service support. The ARTISAN 3D (Advanced Radar Target Indication Situational Awareness and Navigation) is a modular open architecture maritime radar system designed to deal with complex littoral environments. It is being incrementally installed from 2011 as part of the Capability Sustainment Programme (CSP). The Seawolf missile system is expected to reach the end of its service life around 2018 and will be replaced by the Sea Ceptor between 2015-2021.

In 2014 Babcock was awarded a contract to deliver an off-the-shelf communications electronic support measures (CESM) system to provide an enhanced electronic surveillance capability. The system, Hammerhead, will provide surveillance capability, supporting both tactical indicators and warnings and other tasked requirements. Babcock, teamed with principal subcontractor Argon ST, to deliver a system requiring no development work, to enable rapid replacement of the existing obsolete system on the Type 23s.

The MoD has also begun procurement activity to upgrade the power generation system, switchboards and machinery control and surveillance systems under the Power Generation and MCAS Update programme. This should address existing power generation shortfalls while at the same time ensuring that onboard generation capacity can meet the demands of more power hungry weapons and sensors being introduced under the CSP.

Under current plans ships are scheduled to decommission as follows: ARGYLL (2023); LANCASTER (2024); IRON DUKE (2025); MONMOUTH (2026); MONTROSE (2027); WESTMINSTER (2028); NORTHUMBERLAND (2029); RICHMOND (2030); SOMERSET (2031); SUTHERLAND (2033); KENT (2034); PORTLAND (2035) and ST. ALBANS (2036).

HMS Cattistock

MINE COUNTERMEASURES SHIPS (MCMV)
HUNT CLASS

Ship	Pennant Number	Completion Date	Builder
LEDBURY	M30	1981	Vosper T.
CATTISTOCK	M31	1982	Vosper T.
BROCKLESBY	M33	1983	Vosper T.
MIDDLETON	M34	1984	Yarrow
CHIDDINGFOLD	M37	1984	Vosper T.
ATHERSTONE	M38	1987	Vosper T.
HURWORTH	M39	1985	Vosper T.
QUORN	M41	1989	Vosper T.

Displacement 750 tonnes **Dimensions** 60m x 10.5m x 3.4m **Speed** 15 knots **Armament** 1 x 30mm + 2 x Miniguns **Complement** 45

Notes

The largest warships ever built of glass reinforced plastic. Their cost (£35m each) has dictated the size of the class. Very sophisticated ships - and lively seaboats! All are based at Portsmouth as the Second Mine Countermeasures Squadron (MCM2).

BAE Systems has been awarded a six-year contract worth £15m to replace the propulsion systems on these ships, with the work to be carried out at Portsmouth. The first new propulsion system, comprising two Caterpillar C32 engines (replacing the older Napier Deltics) has been installed on board CHIDDINGFOLD which returned to service in 2013. Upgrades to the remaining seven ships will take place during planned ship docking periods up to 2016. The re-propulsion project will involve the installation of new engines, gearboxes, bow thruster systems, propellers and machinery control systems.

In order to keep up the overseas deployment tempo, crews are swapped between ships. ATHERSTONE and CHIDDINGFOLD are forward deployed to the Gulf. QUORN returned to the UK in September 2014 after three years in the Gulf, having been replaced by CHIDDINGFOLD which left Portsmouth in June 2014.

In 2013 the 9th MCM Squadron was stood up at Bahrain, comprising those vessels deployed to the Gulf in support of mine countermeasures operations. Those ships will be identified by a squadron funnel emblem depicting a traditional dhow, resurrecting the identity of the Ton class vessels deployed to the Gulf in the 1960s and 1970s as 9th MSS and latterly 9th MCMS.

Published decommissioning dates are LEDBURY (2019), CATTISTOCK, BROCKLESBY, CHIDDINGFOLD and MIDDLETON (2020), HURWORTH and ATHERSTONE (2022) and QUORN (2023). This is at odds with a press release from the RN on MIDDLETONs return to service in 2014 following her refit and diesel replacement. It was stated that the new engines mean that MIDDLETON can sail faster, stay at sea longer, and will extend the ship's life to 2030 and beyond.

As part of the wider Mine Countermeasures Hydrographic (MHC) programme – intended to deliver a replacement for the RN's mine warfare and hydrographic capabilities – the so-called MHC Sweep Capability project plans the introduction of a new remote control minesweeping system for deployment from the Hunt class - the Hunt class lost its minesweeping capability when the sweep wires and associated equipment were removed in 2005. HAZARD, an optionally manned surface craft that shall be able to venture into minefields to launch and recover unmanned underwater vehicles to search, locate and dispose of mines, can also be used to tow combined influence sweep gear. The concept is being tested by the Maritime Autonomous Systems Trials Team (MASTT) around Portsmouth. It is ultimately envisaged that a full scale demonstration, in the 2018-19 timeframe, could see a Hunt class converted for the launch and recovery of such vessels via an 'A' frame at the stern.

HMS Pembroke

SANDOWN CLASS

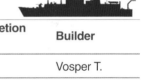

Ship	Pennant Number	Completion Date	Builder
PENZANCE	M106	1998	Vosper T.
PEMBROKE	M107	1998	Vosper T.
GRIMSBY	M108	1999	Vosper T.
BANGOR	M109	2000	Vosper T.
RAMSEY	M110	2000	Vosper T.
BLYTH	M111	2001	Vosper T.
SHOREHAM	M112	2001	Vosper T.

Displacement 600 tons **Dimensions** 52.5m x 109.m x 2m **Speed** 13 knots **Armament** 1 - 30mm gun; 2 x Miniguns; 3 x GPMG **Complement** 34

Notes

A class dedicated to a single mine hunting role. Propulsion is by vectored thrust and bow thrusters. All are based at Faslane as the First Mine Countermeasures Squadron (MCM1). The ships are manned by eight numbered crews which are rotated throughout the squadron allowing deployed vessels to remain on station for extended periods. PENZANCE and SHOREHAM are forward deployed to the Gulf, RAMSEY having returned to the UK in August 2014.

HMS Mersey

PATROL VESSELS
RIVER CLASS

Ship	Pennant Number	Completion Date	Builder
TYNE	P281	2002	Vosper T.
SEVERN	P282	2003	Vosper T.
MERSEY	P283	2003	Vosper T.

Displacement 1,677 tonnes **Dimensions** 79.5m x 13.6m x 3.8m **Speed** 20+ knots
Armament 1 x 20mm; 2 x GPMG **Complement** 48

Notes

Ordered on 8 May 2001, the deal was unusual in that the ships were leased from Vospers (VT) for five years under a £60 million contract. In January 2007 a £52 million lease-contract extension was awarded extending their RN service to the end of 2013. In September 2012 Whitehall signed a £39m contract to buy the ships outright, keeping them in service with the RN for the next ten years. The River class are now the only RN ships permanently conducting Fishery Protection patrols in the waters around England, Wales and Northern Ireland. In the autumn of 2014 SEVERN deployed to the Caribbean to take over the Atlantic Patrol Task (North), the first time an OPV has been deployed on this operation. On station she will be on stand-by for disaster relief operations and any other duties in support of the region's British Overseas Territories, as well as embarking a law enforcement detachment from the US Coast Guard during counter-narcotics operations. It is likely that this is a 'concept proving' deployment in advance of the new Batch II River class entering service.

HMS Clyde

BATCH II RIVER CLASS

Ship	Pennant Number	Completion Date	Builder
CLYDE	P257	2006	VT Shipbuilding

Displacement 1,847 tonnes **Dimensions** 81.5m x 13.6m x 4.15m **Speed** 19 knots (full load) 21 knots (sprint) **Aircraft** Flight Deck to take Lynx, Sea King or Merlin Helicopter **Armament** 1 - 30mm gun; 5 x GPMG; 2 x Minigun **Complement** 36 (space for additional 20 personnel - see note)

Notes

Designed to carry out patrol duties around the Falkland Islands and their dependencies, the ship is able to accommodate a single helicopter up to Merlin size. She deployed to the Falklands in August 2007. CLYDE's more modern design has enabled her to remain on task in the South Atlantic until later this year. Like the previous River class, she had been leased from BAE Systems, for a period of five years. In July 2011 it was announced that BAE Systems had been awarded a six-year contract extension to deliver support services to the ship until 2018. The annual cost to the public purse of operating the ship is £3.5 million.

CLYDE is able to embark a Military Force of up to 110 personnel (the size of the Roulement Infantry Company (RIC)) and move them around the Falkland Islands, inserting them at will.

HMS Scimitar

SCIMITAR CLASS

Ship	Pennant Number	Completion Date	Builder
SCIMITAR	P284	1988	Halmatic
SABRE	P285	1988	Halmatic

Displacement 18.5 tons   **Dimensions** 16m x 4.7m x 1.4m   **Speed** 27+ knots
Armament 2 x GPMG   **Complement** 4

Notes

Assigned to the Royal Navy Gibraltar Squadron (RNGS) the vessels provide Force Protection to visiting coalition warships, maritime security patrols within British Gibraltar Territorial Waters and supports a variety of operations within the Joint Operating Area. In recent years the craft have been facing increasingly provocative stand-offs with their Spanish counterparts in the Guardia Civil as Spain tries to assert its influence over, what it views as, disputed waters in the Bay of Gibraltar. In response additional RN personnel have been deployed to Gibraltar, increasing the number of crews from two to three. RNGS also operate up to three Rigid Hull Inflatable Boats supported by two 15 metre launches and three Arctic 24 RHIBS operated by the Gibraltar Defence Police.

HMS Puncher

COASTAL TRAINING CRAFT
P2000 CLASS

Ship	Pennant Number	Completion Date	Builder
EXPRESS	P163	1988	Vosper T.
EXPLORER	P164	1985	Watercraft
EXAMPLE	P165	1985	Watercraft
EXPLOIT	P167	1988	Vosper T.
ARCHER	P264	1985	Watercraft
BITER	P270	1985	Watercraft
SMITER	P272	1986	Watercraft
PURSUER	P273	1988	Vosper T.
TRACKER	P274	1998	Ailsa Troon
RAIDER	P275	1998	Ailsa Troon
BLAZER	P279	1988	Vosper T.
DASHER	P280	1988	Vosper T.

Ship	Pennant Number	Completion Date	Builder
PUNCHER	P291	1988	Vosper T.
CHARGER	P292	1988	Vosper T.
RANGER	P293	1988	Vosper T.
TRUMPETER	P294	1988	Vosper T.

Displacement 54 tonnes **Dimensions** 20m x 5.8m x 1.9m **Speed** 20 knots **Armament** 3 x GPMG (Faslane based vessels) **Complement** 5 (with accommodation for up to 12 undergraduates).

Notes

Fourteen P2000 craft form the First Patrol Boat Squadron, whose primary role is to support the University Royal Naval Units (URNU) but also contribute to a wide range of Fleet tasking. Commodore Britannia Royal Naval College has overall responsibility for the URNUs whose role is to educate and inform a wide spectrum of high calibre undergraduates. Vessels are assigned to the following URNUs: ARCHER (East Scotland); BITER (Manchester & Salford); BLAZER (Southampton); CHARGER (Liverpool); DASHER (Bristol); EXAMPLE (Northumbria); EXPLOIT (Birmingham); EXPLORER (Yorkshire); EXPRESS (Wales); PUNCHER (London); PURSUER (Glasgow & Strathclyde); RANGER (Sussex); SMITER (Oxford); TRUMPETER (Cambridge).

The last two vessels built, RAIDER and TRACKER, have a higher top speed of 24 knots as they are fitted with two MTU V12 diesels. They now comprise the Faslane Patrol Boat Squadron. Formed in March 2010, the Squadron provides Force Protection in and around Faslane, Scotland. Initially PURSUER and DASHER were relocated to HMNB Clyde from Cyprus in April 2010, arriving at their new home on 6 May that year. They were replaced by RAIDER and TRACKER in September 2012. They are fully-fledged armed patrol boats. Fitted with Kevlar armour and able to mount three 7.62mm General Purpose Machine Guns (GPMG) they are part of a growing Force Protection cadre based at Faslane to protect the UKs nuclear deterrent. These two vessels are fully engaged in FP duties and do not undertake university training.

The P2000s engines are being replaced by two CAT C18 Acert units to help reduce emissions, lower fuel consumption and improve efficiency. BITER was the first to be fitted during an extended refit, to be followed by EXPLORER, RANGER and EXPRESS. The programme, which will cover the entire 16- strong class will extend their lives by 15 years.

HMS Scott

SURVEY SHIPS
SCOTT CLASS

Ship	Pennant Number	Completion Date	Builder
SCOTT	H131	1997	Appledore

Displacement 13,300 tonnes **Dimensions** 131.5m x 21.5m x 9m **Speed** 17 knots
Complement 63 (42 embarked at any one time)

Notes

Designed to commercial standards SCOTT provides the RN with a deep bathymetric capability off the continental shelf. Fitted with a modern multi-beam sonar suite she can conduct mapping of the ocean floor worldwide. She carries a mixture of the latest UK and US survey equipment. She operates a three watch system whereby the vessel is run by 42 of her ship's company of 63 - with the remainder on leave. Each crew member works 75 days in the ship before having 30 days off, allowing her to spend more than 300 days at sea in a year. Extensive use of commercial lean manning methods including unmanned machinery spaces, fixed fire fighting systems and extensive machinery and safety surveillance technology. Her hull is Ice class 1A: Ships with such structure, engine output and other properties are capable of navigating in difficult ice conditions, but only with the assistance of icebreakers. In 2013 Babcock won a five year contract from the MoD to provide through life engineering support to the ship. In November 2013 SCOTT began a drydocking and upgrade period at Devonport, during which she received a number of upgrades and improvements, including a new sewage treatment plant and new lifeboat davits, as well as a new uninterrupted power supply to the ship's sonar suite. She left drydock in June 2014.

ECHO CLASS

Ship	Pennant Number	Completion Date	Builder
ECHO	H87	2002	Appledore
ENTERPRISE	H88	2003	Appledore

Displacement 3,500 tonnes **Dimensions** 90m x 16.8m x 5.5.m **Speed** 15 knots **Armament** 2 x 20mm **Complement** 49 (with accommodation for 81)

Notes

In June 2000, a £130 million order was placed with prime contractor Vosper Thornycroft to build and maintain, over a 25 year period, these two new Survey Vessels Hydrographic Oceanographic (SVHO). Both vessels were built by sub-contractor Appledore Shipbuilding Limited. They have a secondary role as mine countermeasures HQ ships. The total ship's company is 72, with 48 personnel onboard at any one time working a cycle of 75 days on, 30 days off, allowing the ships to be operationally available for 330 days a year. Utilizing a diesel electric propulsion system, they have three main generators. They are the first RN ships to be fitted with Azimuth pod thrusters in place of the more normal shaft and propellor. Each ship carries a named survey launch, SAPPHIRE (ECHO) and SPITFIRE (ENTERPRISE). SPITFIRE is a new design 9m SMB powered by two 6-cylinder diesels linked to jet propulsion units. It is equipped with side scan sonar and both multi-beam and single beam echo sounders. In November 2014, ECHO, nearing the end of an 18-month deployment, conducted an unscheduled drydocking in Gibraltar. ENTERPRISE sailed from Devonport in June 2014 at the start of an extended deployment.

HMS Gleaner

INSHORE SURVEY VESSEL

Ship	Pennant Number	Completion Date	Builder
GLEANER	H86	1983	Emsworth

Displacement 26 tons **Dimensions** 14.8m x 4.7m x 1.6m **Speed** 14 knots
Complement 8

Notes

Small inshore survey craft used for the collection of data from the shallowest inshore waters. She uses multi-beam and sidescan sonar to collect bathymetry and seabed texture data and compile an accurate and detailed picture of the seabed. She was scheduled to decommission in 2007, but she emerged, in 2008, from a Service Life Extension Programme, which will enable her to remain in service for a further 10 years. She carries the prefix Her Majesty's Survey Motor Launch or HMSML.

Four small survey boats, NESBITT, PAT BARTON, COOK and OWEN are attached to the Hydrographic School at Devonport.

HMS Protector

ICE PATROL SHIPS
PROTECTOR

Ship	Pennant Number	Completion Date	Builder
PROTECTOR	A173	2001	Havyard Leirvik (Norway)

Displacement 4,985 tons **Dimensions** 89.7m x 18m x 7.25m **Speed** 15 knots
Armament Miniguns; GPMGs **Complement** 88

Notes

The ice-breaker MV POLARBJORN was initially leased, in June 2011, on a three-year contract from the Norwegian company GC Rieber Shipping as a temporary replacement for the damaged ENDURANCE and commissioned as PROTECTOR. In 2013 it was announced that the ship had been purchased by the MoD. Oddly, it was also announced in July 2014, as part of a defence spending package, that PROTECTOR was to be purchased! Although the ship has a flight deck, there is no hangar, so she will be unable to deploy with an embarked helicopter. She operates the Survey Motor Boat JAMES CAIRD IV and the 8.5 metre Rigid Work Boat TERRA NOVA. She can also deploy two Pacific 22 RIBs (NIMROD and AURORA). She also deploys with three BV206 all terrain vehicles and four quad bikes and trailers to assist in moving stores and equipment. On 17 October 2013 she sailed from Portsmouth, for the last time, for a double deployment to Antarctica. The ship will stay in the region for two consecutive deployments, returning to her new home at Devonport Naval Base in Spring 2015, where she will be based with the rest of the Hydrographic fleet.

ENDURANCE

Ship	Pennant Number	Completion Date	Builder
ENDURANCE	A171	1990	Ulstein-Hatlo

Displacement 5,129 tons **Dimensions** 91m x 17.9m x 6.5m **Speed** 14.9 knots
Armament Small arms **Aircraft** 2 Lynx **Complement** 116

Notes

Originally MV POLAR CIRCLE she was chartered for 7 months in 1991 to replace the original ENDURANCE. She was renamed HMS POLAR CIRCLE (A176) before being purchased by the MoD and renamed ENDURANCE in October 1992. Historically she spent 4-6 months each year in the South Atlantic supporting the British Antarctic Survey. Following a flooding incident off Chile in 2008 she was returned to the UK aboard a heavylift ship in April 2009. She has remained at Portsmouth ever since. In 2013 it was announced that PROTECTOR had been bought as a permanent replacement and that ENDURANCE would be withdrawn from service in 2015. The wording of the announcement was odd considering that the ship has been deteriorating at Portsmouth since being returned in 2009 and could never be considered as being "in service". Hopefully this year will see the ship finally disposed of.

ROYAL MARINE CRAFT

In August 2013 the Royal Marines concentrated their various assault and landing craft at a newly built facility, housed at Devonport Naval Base. RM Tamar, as it is now known, is home to the RMs Landing Craft, Hovercraft and other vessels when not required for deployment, either onboard the assault ships, or independently.

Based at RM Tamar is 1 Assault Group Royal Marines (1 AGRM), the lead for amphibious warfare and Royal Navy board and search training. The group is tasked with training and developing core amphibious and surface assault skills and equipment, including the provision of operational support for the Ministry of Defence.

1 AGRM is responsible for 4 subordinate units which deliver the vast spectrum of training and operations required in delivering amphibious and surface assault capability of the Royal Navy and Royal Marines.

10 (Landing Craft) Training Squadron - Responsible for delivering landing craftsmen training as well as small boats, engineering and assault navigation training.

11 Amphibious Trials and Training Squadron (Instow, North Devon) - Delivering training that covers the area between the craft and the beachhead. The Instow squadron also conducts the trials and testing of future craft.

The Royal Navy School of Board and Search at HMS Raleigh in Torpoint trains both individuals and ship's boarding teams to conduct the full range of boarding operations that is required by the Naval Service.

In addition, 1AGRM is also tasked with parenting the Assault Squadrons of the Royal Marines (ASRMs) and their Landing Craft detachments which are assigned to the amphibious assault ships. These ASRMs provide the landing craft and therefore the fighting capability for the RN's Amphibious Ships, OCEAN (9 ASRM); ALBION (6 ASRM - currently disbanded and operated as 6 Ops Sqn until ALBION returns to service) and BULWARK (4 ASRM).

43 Commando Fleet Protection Group Royal Marines (43 Cdo FP Gp RM) is based at HM Naval Base Clyde near Helensburgh on the West Coast of Scotland. Formerly Comacchio Group it was renamed in April 2012 and, together with 539 ASRM, became part of 3 Commando Brigade. The Group's core task is to provide military support to undertake final denial of access to nuclear weapons in addition to supporting the multi-agency force that protects nuclear weapons convoys. Additionally, specially trained teams are deployed at short notice to conduct tasks in support of the RN worldwide. Tasks have ranged from Force Protection, to conducting non-compliant boarding operations and counter-piracy operations.

Mull

ISLAND CLASS PATROL VESSELS

Ship	Pennant Number	Launch Date	Builder
RONA	-	2009	Holyhead Marine
MULL	-	2010	Holyhead Marine

Displacement 19.9 tonnes **Dimensions** 14.9m x 4.1m x 0.9m **Speed** 33 knots
Armament 4 x GPMG **Complement** 4

Notes

Originally units of a class of five launches delivered to the Ministry of Defence Police, RONA and MULL were transferred to 43 Commando Fleet Protection Group Royal Marines for operation on the Clyde to escort high value units. The vessels were returned to Holyhead Marine where they were modified in December 2012 and January 2013 respectively. As well as major reworking of their upper decks, the vessels were fitted with three new weapon mounts, enhanced protection for coxswains and crew, as well as an enhanced communications package.

LCU Mk10 B3

LCU Mk10

Ship	Pennant Number	Parent Unit	Builder
9730	P1	10 Trg Sqn, TAMAR	Ailsa, Troon
9731	P2	11 ATT Sqn, INSTOW	Ailsa, Troon
9732	A1	6 Ops Sqn, TAMAR	BAE Systems
9733	B2	HMS BULWARK	BAE Systems
9734	A2	10 Trg Sqn, TAMAR	BAE Systems
9735	B3	HMS BULWARK	BAE Systems
9736	A4	HMS BULWARK	BAE Systems
9737	B1	HMS BULWARK	BAE Systems
9738	B3	6 Ops Sqn, TAMAR	BAE Systems
9739	FJ	10 Trg Sqn, TAMAR	BAE Systems

Displacement 240 tonnes **Dimensions** 29.82m x 7.7m x 1.70m **Speed** 8.5 knots **Armament** 2 x GPMG **Complement** 7

Notes

Ro-Ro style landing craft designed to operate from the Albion class LPDs or Landing Ship Dock Auxiliary (LSD(A)). Ordered in 1998 from Ailsa Troon. The first two were delivered in 1999 with the final vessels being accepted into service in 2003. The remainder were built by BAE Systems at Govan. Capable of lifting one Main Battle Tank or four lighter vehicles. Capacity for 100 fully equipped troops. With a range of around 600 nautical miles – more if auxiliary tanks are added – is designed to operate independently for 14 days with its seven man Royal Marine crew in both arctic and tropical climates. All the crew members have bunk accommodation and there is a galley and store rooms. Unlike other vessels, pennant numbers and parent units can change as the vessels are rotated through maintenance cycles.

LCVP Mk5B B6

LCVP Mk5A/5B

Ship	Pennant Number	Parent Unit	Builder
Mk5A			
9707	-	10 Trg Sqn, TAMAR	Babcock Marine
9675	-	10 Trg Sqn, TAMAR	Vosper T.
9676	-	10 Trg Sqn, TAMAR	Vosper T.
Mk5B			
0202	A8	539 ASRM, TAMAR	Babcock Marine
0203	A6	HMS OCEAN	Babcock Marine
0204	A7	539 ASRM, TAMAR	Babcock Marine
0205	A5	10 Trg Sqn, TAMAR	Babcock Marine
0338	T6	11 ATT Sqn, INSTOW	Babcock Marine

Ship	Pennant Number	Parent Unit	Builder
0339	P6	10 Trg Sqn, TAMAR	Babcock Marine
0340	P7	HMS OCEAN	Babcock Marine
0341	P4	10 Trg Sqn, TAMAR	Babcock Marine
0344	NM	HMS BULWARK	Babcock Marine
0345	N2	HMS BULWARK	Babcock Marine
0346	N3	HMS OCEAN	Babcock Marine
0347	N4	HMS OCEAN	Babcock Marine
0353	B6	539 ASRM, TAMAR	Babcock Marine
0354		539 ASRM, TAMAR	Babcock Marine
0355	B7	HMS BULWARK	Babcock Marine
0356	B8	HMS BULWARK	Babcock Marine

Displacement 24 tonnes **Dimensions** 15.70m x 3.5m x 0.90m **Speed** 25 knots **Armament** 2 x GPMG **Complement** 3

Notes

First one ordered in 1995 from Vosper Thornycroft and handed over in 1996. A further four were delivered in December 1996 to operate from OCEAN, with two more for training at RM Poole ordered in 1998. A further 16 were ordered from Babcock in 2001 with the final vessels being accepted into service in 2004. The Mk 5 can lift 8 tonnes of stores or a mix of 2 tonnes and 35 troops. These vessels have a greater range, lift and speed than the Mk4s which they replaced. The primary role is the landing of vehicles, personnel and equipment onto potentially hostile shores. The secondary role is a general purpose support craft both between ships and ship to shore. The craft is capable of performing its normal duties in conditions up to sea state 4 and run for cover up to sea state 5. Pennant numbers and parent units can change as the vessels are rotated through maintenance cycles.

Griffon 2400TD

4 GRIFFON 2400TD LCAC

Ship	Pennant Number	Completion Date	Builder
C23	-	2010	Griffon
C24	-	2010	Griffon
C25	-	2010	Griffon
C26	-	2010	Griffon

G.R.T. 6.8 tons **Dimensions** 13.4m x 6.8m **Speed** 45 knots **Range** 300 nm **Armament** 1 x GPMG **Complement** 2 Crew; 16 fully-equipped marines.

Notes

Operated by 539 Assault Squadron, the 2400TD offers greater payload, performance and obstacle clearance than the earlier 2000 TD craft. Centre sections of the cabin roof can be removed in order to embark two one-tonne NATO pallets. They can be transported on a standard low loader truck or in the hold of a C-130 Hercules aircraft. They can also operate directly from the well-deck of RN amphibious ships. They are equipped with a 7.62mm General Purpose Machine Gun, HF and VHF radios, radar, GPS, ballistic protection and a variety of specialised equipment. All four entered service by the end of 2010.

OFFSHORE RAIDING CRAFT

The Royal Marines operate two versions of the Offshore Raiding Craft (ORC), the Troop Carrying Variant (TCV) and Fire Support Variant (FSV). The ORC is an air portable surface manoeuvre craft designed for the rapid deployment of 8 fully equipped troops and 2 crew from over the horizon (30 miles) ship to shore and vice versa. They provide rapid movement of troops in coastal, estuarine, riverine and inland waters. Specifications: Weight: 3.6 tonnes - Length: 9.1m - Speed: 36 kts - Capacity: 2 Crew + 8 fully equipped troops.

RIGID RAIDING CRAFT

The Royal Marines operate a number of smaller Rigid-hulled and Rigid-Inflatable craft for various assault, patrol and security duties. There are 5.2, 6.5 and 8 metre long versions. Rigid Raiders feature GRP (glass reinforced plastic) hulls and early variants featured single or twin outboard motors. The latest RRC, the Mk3, is powered by an inboard diesel engine. They can carry up to eight troops.

SPECIALIST CRAFT

In addition to the familiar Rigid Raiding Craft and Rigid Inflatable Boats other specialist vessels are available including air transportable Fast Insertion Craft (FIC) with a speed of 55 knots in addition to advanced wave piercing designs. Swimmer Delivery Vehicles (SDV), in reality miniature submarines, which can be deployed from dry deck shelters on larger submarines, are also operated as a part of the UK Special Forces inventory.

Following trials with Swedish CP90 Combat Boats, the Royal Marines were hopeful of procuring a new Force Protection Craft, based on experience with the CB 90s, capable of landing troops and protecting the landing craft from seaborne and land based threats. An in service date of 2016 was anticipated, but to date there has been little indication of progress with this programme.

SHIPS FOR THE FUTURE FLEET

QUEEN ELIZABETH CLASS AIRCRAFT CARRIERS

After a decade of design studies, a contract for the construction of two aircraft carriers, QUEEN ELIZABETH and PRINCE OF WALES, the largest warships to be designed and built in the UK, was signed in July 2008 between the Government and the Aircraft Carrier Alliance, an industrial group comprising BAE Systems Surface Ships, Babcock Marine, Thales and the Ministry of Defence.

The ships are being built in sections constructed by BAE Systems at Govan, Scotstoun and Portsmouth; Babcock in Rosyth and Appledore; Cammell Laird in Birkenhead and A & P, Tyne and are being assembled in Number 1 Dock at Rosyth. The dock at Rosyth has had the entrance widened from 124 feet to 138 feet. The sides were re-profiled with the removal of angled steps to make the dock floor 30 feet wider. A new overhead crane with a span of 394 feet, named Goliath, has been installed to straddle the dock and lift the smaller blocks into place. The individual blocks are built under cover and fitted out with machinery and sub-assemblies such as diesel generators, offices, cabins and galleys before they are moved to Rosyth.

The completed ships will be 284 metres long with a waterline beam of 39 metres and beam across the flight deck of 73 metres. Height from the bottom of the hull to the masthead will be 57.5 metres and draught 11 metres. There are 9 decks in the hull with another 9 in the two islands. Each ship is expected to be in the dock for two years and will be 'floated out' into the adjacent non-tidal basin for completion. The 2010 SDSR determined that the new carriers should operate the conventional F-35C 'tail-hook' variant of the Joint Strike fighter, rather than the intended F-35B STOVL variant and be converted for 'cat & trap' operations. The Conversion Development Phase was scheduled to run to late 2012. However, concerns as to the affordability of the CV conversion prompted the MoD to reconsider the STOVL option in an attempt to finalise its PR12 budget planning round and balance the equipment programme.

According to the MoD, work undertaken had revealed that the CV-capable carrier strike capability would not be ready until 2023, some three years later than originally planned. Furthermore, the cost of fitting the Electromagnetic Aircraft Launch System (EMALS), Advanced Arresting Gear (AAG) and other CV aviation systems into PRINCE OF WALES was now estimated at £2 billion, over double the initial estimate of £950 million.

In his statement to parliament, the Secretary of State for Defence said that the SDSR decision on carriers "was right at the time, but the facts have changed and therefore so too must our approach".

He added: "Carrier strike with 'cats and traps' using the Carrier Variant jet no longer represents the best way of delivering carrier strike and I am not prepared to tolerate a three year further delay to reintroducing our Carrier Strike capability." The MoD initially said that about £40 million had been spent to date on the Carrier Conversion Development Phase. However, he later admitted that the total cost of the u-turn, taking into account other costs and penalties, came to about £100 million.

Her Majesty Queen Elizabeth II formally named the future HMS QUEEN ELIZABETH at Babcock's Rosyth dockyard on 4 July 2014. A little less than a fortnight later, on 17 July, the ship was floated out of No.1 dock at Rosyth dockyard in Fife to an outfitting berth in the adjacent basin. She is scheduled to begin sea trials in 2016.

On 9 September, Lower Block 03 (LB03) and Lower Block 02 (LB02) of PRINCE OF WALES were docked down into the build dock at Rosyth, marking the start of the assembly phase for PRINCE OF WALES. The lower section of the bow, VB01, and the first of the centre blocks completing block 03 up to the flight deck level have now been installed using the Goliath crane.

TYPE 26 FRIGATE (GLOBAL COMBAT SHIP)

Conceived as a multi-mission warship designed for joint and multi-national operations across the full spectrum of warfare, the Type 26 is planned to progressively replace the Type 23 frigates from the early part of the next decade.

The ships will employ a Combined Diesel Electric or Gas Turbine propulsion system. This will enable the ships to achieve high speeds, whilst also providing an economic power to the onboard systems and will allow the ships to operate quietly in cruising mode. Rolls-Royce has been selected as the design partner for Gas Turbines, while David Brown Gear Systems Ltd will develop the Gear box and MTU the Diesel Generator Sets. Rohde & Schwarz has been selected to design the Integrated Communications System for the ships. It is understood that the BAE Systems Mk45 Mod 4 4.5-inch/62-calibre gun has been selected as the main gun system, while the Lockheed Martin Mk 41 VLS system is likely to selected to meet the requirement for a 24-cell Flexible Strike Silo.

The Assessment Phase for the Type 26 programme began in March 2010, with a joint team of 550 engineers from BAE Systems, MoD and wider industry working across Bristol, Portsmouth and Glasgow to develop the detailed specification for the ships.

The MoD is expected to make its Main Investment decision by the end of 2014, with manufacturing planned to start in 2016 and the first Type 26 set to enter service as soon as possible after 2020.

Current plans call for a class of 13 ships to replace the current Type 23s on a one-for-one basis. However, it has been stated that the first order will be for an initial 8 ships and towards the end of 2014, statements in parliament were already refering to a class of "up to" 13 ships.

BATCH 2 RIVER CLASS

Steel was cut, on 10 October 2014, for the first of three new Batch 2 River class offshore patrol vessels, HMS FORTH, at a ceremony in Glasgow. The plan to build three OPVs was announced in November 2013 and a manufacturing contract was placed with BAE Systems in August 2014.

The ships, based on the 90m vessels in service with Brazil and Thailand, have been ordered as part of a deal to sustain key industrial capabilities between the completion of the Queen Elizabeth-class carriers and the start of the Type 26 programme. At £348 million (compared to £150 million for the three Brazilian Amazonas class) these are very expensive vessels - being built to keep a shipyard in work rather than for any operational imperative.

The basic design has been modified to meet specific RN requirements including a strengthened flight deck to operate a Merlin helicopter; modified and uprated helicopter in-flight refuelling arrangements; additional accommodation for embarked military detachments and improved watertight integrity and firefighting equipment. At 2,000-tonnes the ship will have a range of 5,000 miles and could be deployed in support of UK interests both at home and abroad. The ships will be armed with a single MSI-Defence Systems 30mm gun and two Mk 44 mini-guns. She will also be fitted with a variant of BAE's CMS-1 combat management system and a SCANTER 4103 I-band radar.

HMS FORTH is expected to begin sea trials in 2016 and be handed over in spring 2017. The second, to be named MEDWAY, will be delivered in October 2017 and the third, to be named TRENT, in July 2018.

MILITARY AFLOAT REACH AND SUSTAINABILITY (MARS)

The future re-equipment of the RFA rests with this programme in which it is envisioned 11 ships will be procured (Five fleet tankers - delivered 2011 to 2015; Three joint sea-based logistics vessels - 2016, 2017 and 2020; Two fleet solid-support ships - 2017 and 2020 and a single fleet tanker - 2021).

At the end of 2007 the MoD invited industry to express their interest in the project to build up to six fleet tankers. In May 2008 four companies had been shortlisted to submit proposals for the design and construction of the ships however, this project was deferred in December 2008, the MoD announcing that having reviewed all the components of the MARS fleet auxiliary programme it was concluded that there was scope for considering alternative approaches to its procurement. Post SDSR the government stated that the requirement for the MARS programme is driven by the logistic support needs of the future RN; these being assessed following the outcome of the SDSR. It now seems likely that MARS will deliver just seven vessels (four tankers and up to three solid-support ships).

In February 2012 the MoD announced that Daewoo Shipbuilding and Marine Engineering (DSME) of South Korea were the preferred bidder in a £425 million contract to build four 37,000 tonne tankers for the RFA, the first of which is planned to enter service in 2016. They will form a new Tide class, being named TIDESPRING, TIDERACE, TIDESURGE and TIDEFORCE. DSME are drawing up detailed plans to begin construction, at Okpo-dong, south-east Korea, in 2014 .

The principal particulars of the design include an overall length of 200.9 metres, a breadth of 28.6 metres, a draught of 10 metres, and a displacement (full load) of just over 37,000 tonnes. Replenishment facilities comprise: three abeam RAS(L) stations (two sited starboard and one to port) for diesel oil, aviation fuel and fresh water; solid RAS reception up to 2 tonnes; and vertical replenishment using an embarked helicopter (the design features a flight deck sized for a Merlin, a maintenance hangar, and an in-flight refuelling capability). Provision is also made for the future fit of a stern fuel delivery reel.

The building of the first vessel, TIDESPRING, began in South Korea in June 2014, with the building of each vessel scheduled to take 10 months. She is scheduled to be delivered to the MOD on 15 October 2015 for final fitting out of sensitive equipment, followed by the others at six monthly intervals - the final delivery being planned for 15 April 2017.

With the tanker programme now under contract, the MoD is turning its attention towards the other MARS component in the shape of the Future Solid Support (FSS) programme. This second element of the modernisation of the RFA is intended to introduce replacements for RFAs FORT AUSTIN, FORT ROSALIE and FORT VICTORIA from the early 2020s.

The FSS design will deliver bulk ammunition, dry stores and food to support both carrier strike and littoral manoeuvre operations. Current plans assume a total of three FSS vessels, each displacing approximately 40,000 tonnes.

SUCCESSOR SUBMARINE PROGRAMME

The Successor programme envisages the delivery of three or four SSBNs to replace the RN's four existing Vanguard-class submarines from 2028 to maintain continuous at-sea deterrence (CASD). Initial gate approval was announced by the MoD in May 2011, marking the transition from the programme's concept phase to the current assessment phase. Assessment phase activities will finalise the Successor design, fund long lead items and start industrialisation to support manufacture. However, the key main gate investment decision - which will commit to construction and also determine whether CASD can be delivered by three or four boats - will not be taken until 2016, which is when the Government will decide whether or not to approve full production.

Work on the concept design phase for a submarine to replace the Vanguard class has been ongoing since 2007, but this has now been completed, and an outline submarine design has been selected. Work with the US on a Common Missile Compartment is ongoing to evaluate how best to incorporate the UK's requirement for eight operational missiles, against a baseline design for the CMC which currently involves a 12 missile tube unit. It has been recognised that the cost of the CMC will be minimised by keeping as much of the design as possible in common with the US.

In 2012 two contracts worth £350 million each were awarded by the MoD to enable detailed design work to continue on both the submarine design and the new PWR3 nuclear reactor. Although a decision on the final design and build will not be made until 2016, detailed work has to take place now to ensure that the Successor submarines can begin to be delivered in 2028.

THE ROYAL FLEET AUXILIARY

The Royal Fleet Auxiliary (RFA) is a civilian manned fleet, owned by the Ministry of Defence. Traditionally, its main task has been to replenish warships of the Royal Navy at sea with fuel, food, stores and ammunition to extend their operations away from base support. However, as the RN surface fleet has shrunk, the RFA has shrunk with it but it has also acted as a 'force multiplier' being able to take on some operational roles. By embarking helicopters, tankers and stores ships have been deployed on RN patrol tasks in the Caribbean and on counter-piracy operations. By embarking ASW helicopters they are also able to provide additional warfare support to task group operations. Like the RN, the RFA are suffering manpower shortages, particularly in the engineering specialisation, and it has been noticeable that at least three ships have spent extended periods along-side in 2014, reportedly laid-up due to lack of engineering staff, although the MoD are keen to confirm that those ships remain in the operational cycle.

Legislation banning the use of single-hulled tankers in 2010 is driving the need for replacement ships. There are three such dedicated tankers in-service with the RFA with a further general replenishment ship that has a tanking capability. However, such is the delay in the new tanker programme that the two Rover class tankers have had their service lives extended by a further seven years - making them 42 years old before they are expected to finally pay off. RFA GOLD ROVER commenced her final operational deployment in 2014 and is expected to be replaced by the first of the Tide class on her return.

As part of the Military Afloat Reach and Sustainability (MARS) programme, the MoD placed an order in 2012 for four tankers to be built in South Korea. They will be named TIDESPRING, TIDERACE, TIDESURGE and TIDEFORCE (see page 45).

The long term maintenance of the RFA fleet rests with shipyards in the North West, North East and South West of England. Cammell Laird Shiprepairers & Shipbuilders Ltd of Birkenhead and the A&P Group in Falmouth and Newcastle-upon-Tyne were named as the contractors to maintain the flotilla of 16 RFA tankers, stores and landing ships. They maintain 'clusters' of ships, providing the necessary refuelling and refit work for the RFA vessels throughout their service lives. Ships are grouped in clusters according to their duties and capabilities. A&P Group are charged with two clusters (Cluster 1: ARGUS and Cluster 2: CARDIGAN BAY, LYME BAY, MOUNTS BAY) in a contract worth around £53 million with the work to be shared between its bases in Falmouth and on the Tyne, while CL Ltd is contracted for the maintenance of four clusters of ships (Cluster 3: ORANGE-LEAF, BLACK ROVER, GOLD ROVER; Cluster 4: DILIGENCE, WAVE KNIGHT, WAVE RULER; Cluster 5: FORT AUSTIN, FORT ROSALIE and Cluster 6: FORT VICTORIA).

SHIPS OF THE ROYAL FLEET AUXILIARY
Pennant Numbers

Ship	Pennant Number	Page	Ship	Pennant Number	Page
Tankers			**Amphibious Ships**		
ORANGELEAF	A110	51	LYME BAY	L3007	55
GOLD ROVER	A271	52	MOUNTS BAY	L3008	55
BLACK ROVER	A273	52	CARDIGAN BAY	L3009	55
WAVE KNIGHT	A389	50			
WAVE RULER	A390	50	**Repair Ship**		
			DILIGENCE	A132	56
Stores Ships					
FORT ROSALIE	A385	53	**Primary Casualty Receiving**		
FORT AUSTIN	A386	53	**Ship/Aviation Training Ship**		
			ARGUS	A135	57
Stores Ship/Tankers					
FORT VICTORIA	A387	54			

RFA Wave Knight

FAST FLEET TANKERS

WAVE CLASS

Ship	Pennant Number	Completion Date	Builder
WAVE KNIGHT	A 389	2002	BAe Systems
WAVE RULER	A 390	2002	BAe Systems

Displacement 31,500 tons (Full Load) **Dimensions** 196 x 27 x 10m **Speed** 18 knots **Armament** 2 x Vulcan Phalanx, 2 x 30mm **Aircraft** Up to 2 Merlin **Complement** 80 (plus 22 Fleet Air Arm)

Notes

These 31,500-tonne ships are diesel-electric powered, with three refuelling rigs. They have a cargo capacity of 16,900 tonnes (Fuel) and 915 tonnes (Dry Stores). They have a large one spot flight deck, hangar and maintenance facilities capable of supporting two Merlin helicopters. They have spent extended periods in the Caribbean conducting successful counter-narcotics operations with an embarked RN helicopter.

RFA Orangeleaf

SUPPORT TANKERS
LEAF CLASS

Ship	Pennant Number	Completion Date	Builder
ORANGELEAF	A110	1982	Cammell Laird

Displacement 37,747 tons **Dimensions** 170m x 26m x 12m **Speed** 14.5 knots **Complement** 60

Notes

A single-hulled ex-merchant ship, originally acquired for employment mainly on freighting duties. A commercial Stat32 class tanker modified to enable it to refuel warships at sea. In 2007 she completed a Service Life Extension Programme (SLEP) refit which will enable her planned decommissioning in 2015. She arrived at Birkenhead in June for a maintenance period and has remained there since, reportedly laid up for a period of 12 months, which will effectively see her through to decommissioning.

The MoD also has the commercial tanker MAERSK RAPIER under charter. She is a multi-tasked tanker which supplies fuel to the naval facilities in the UK and abroad. The MoD charters the vessel to commercial companies when it is not in use for their own requirements. The tanker MT CUMBRIAN FISHER has also been occasionally chartered for moving fuel products between the UK and the Falkland Islands.

RFA Gold Rover

SMALL FLEET TANKERS

ROVER CLASS

Ship	Pennant Number	Completion Date	Builder
GOLD ROVER	A271	1974	Swan Hunter
BLACK ROVER	A273	1974	Swan Hunter

Displacement 11,522 tons **Dimensions** 141m x 19m x 7m **Speed** 18 knots **Armament** 2 - 20mm guns **Complement** 49/54

Notes

Small Fleet Tankers designed to supply warships with fresh water, dry cargo and refrigerated provisions, as well as a range of fuels and lubricants. Helicopter deck, but no hangar. Have been employed in recent years mainly as support for HM Ships operating around the Falkland Islands and as the FOST station tanker. Now over 40 years old, GOLD ROVER sailed to the South Atlantic for her final deployment in September 2014. On her return in 2016 she will be decommissioned. BLACK ROVER returned to the UK in November 2014 following a 17-month deployment to the South Atlantic. She is scheduled to decommission in 2017.

• CAPTAIN S. JONES OBE RFA   **RFA Fort Austin**

STORES VESSELS
FORT CLASS I

Ship	Pennant Number	Completion Date	Builder
FORT ROSALIE	A385	1978	Scott Lithgow
FORT AUSTIN	A386	1979	Scott Lithgow

Displacement 23,384 tons **Dimensions** 183m x 24m x 9m **Armament** 2 x Vulcan Phalanx **Speed** 20 knots **Complement** 201, (120 RFA, 36 MoD Civilians & 45 Fleet Air Arm)

Notes

Full hangar and maintenance facilities are provided and up to four Sea King or Lynx helicopters can be carried for both the transfer of stores and anti-submarine protection of a group of ships (note: these ships are not cleared to operate Merlin). Both ships can be armed with 4 - 20mm guns. FORT AUSTIN received two Vulcan Phalanx mounts sited to port and starboard above the bridge wings. FORT ROSALIE entered a 22-week refit at Birkenhead in January 2013 and has remained there since. Again it is reported that she has been laid up for 12-months. FORT AUSTIN is scheduled to decommission in 2021 and FORT ROSALIE in 2022.

RFA Fort Victoria

REPLENISHMENT SHIPS
FORT CLASS II

Ship	Pennant Number	Completion Date	Builder
FORT VICTORIA	A387	1992	Harland & Wolff

Displacement 35,500 tons **Dimensions** 204m x 30m x 9m **Speed** 20 knots **Armament** 4 - 30mm guns, 2 x Phalanx CIWS, Sea Wolf Missile System (Fitted for but not with) **Complement** 100 (RFA), 24 MoD Civilians, 32 RN and up to 122 Fleet Air Arm

Notes

A "One stop" replenishment ship with the widest range of armaments, fuel and spares carried. Can operate up to 5 Sea King/Lynx or 3 Merlin Helicopters (more in a ferry role) with full maintenance facilities onboard. Medical facilities were upgraded with a 12 bed surgical capability. Under current plans she is to remain in service until 2019. She returned to the UK on 9 December 2013 following a 1,197 day deployment to the Gulf. She arrived at Cammell Laird, Birkenhead, in March 2014 at the start of a £47million refit. She is scheduled to return to service in early 2015.

RFA Lyme Bay

LANDING SHIP DOCK (AUXILIARY) BAY CLASS

Ship	Pennant Number	Completion Date	Builder
LYME BAY	L3007	2007	Swan Hunter
MOUNTS BAY	L3008	2006	BAe Systems
CARDIGAN BAY	L3009	2007	BAe Systems

Displacement 16,190 tonnes **Dimensions** 176.6m x 26.4m x 5.1m **Speed** 18 knots
Armament 2 x Vulcan Phalanx in some **Complement** 60

Notes

The dock is capable of operating LCU 10s and they carry two LCVP Mk5s. They can offload at sea, over the horizon. In addition to their war fighting role they could be well suited to disaster relief and other humanitarian missions. Since 2010, vessels emerging from refit have received two funnels running up the side of the midships gantry. These were resited due to problems with fumes over the aft end of the flightdeck. Additional mini-gun emplacements have been added at the stern (in place of the aft funnels) and amidships. CARDIGAN BAY is deployed to the Gulf and is fitted with two Phalanx CIWS mounts to port and starboard. LYME BAY emerged from refit with Phalanx mounts sited forward of the superstructure and on top of the aft end of the superstructure. She deployed as part of the Cougar 2014 Task Group fitted with a temporary aircraft shelter aft of the superstructure. In December 2013 MOUNTS BAY arrived at Falmouth for maintenance following the Cougar Deployment. She remained alongside throughout 2014.

RFA Diligence

FORWARD REPAIR SHIP

Ship	Pennant Number	Completion Date	Builder
DILIGENCE	A132	1981	Oesundsvarvet

Displacement 10,595 tons **Dimensions** 120m x 12m x 3m **Speed** 15 knots **Armament** 2 - 20mm **Complement** RFA 40, RN Personnel - approx 100

Notes

Formerly the MV STENA INSPECTOR purchased (£25m) for service in the South Atlantic. Her deep diving complex was removed. She is fitted with a wide range of workshops for hull and machinery repairs, as well as facilities for supplying electricity, water, fuel, air, steam, cranes and stores to other ships and submarines. When not employed on battle repair duties she can serve as a support vessel for MCMVs and submarines on deployment. Deployed as part of the Response Force Task Group in 2013 she remained deployed east of Suez in support of National Tasking until returning to the UK in September 2014 to undertake a refit at Birkenhead.

RFA Argus

PRIMARY CASUALTY RECEIVING SHIP/AVIATION TRAINING SHIP

Ship	Pennant Number	Completion Date	Builder
ARGUS	A135	1981	Cantieri Navali Breda

Displacement 28,481 tons (full load) **Dimensions** 175m x 30m x 8m **Speed** 18 knots **Armament** 4 - 30 mm, 2 - 20 mm **Complement** 254 (inc 137 Fleet Air Arm) **Aircraft** 6 Sea King/Merlin.

Notes

The former MV CONTENDER BEZANT was purchased in 1984 and rebuilt at Harland and Wolff, Belfast, from 1984-87 to operate as an Aviation Training Ship. She undertook a rapid conversion in October 1990 to become a Primary Casualty Receiving Ship (PCRS) for service in the Gulf. These facilities were upgraded and made permanent during 2001. In 2009 the ship underwent a Service Life Extension Programme at Falmouth to switch her primary role to that of PCRS with a secondary aviation training role. The construction of new casualty access lifts together with a new deckhouse aft of the superstructure has reduced helicopter capability by one landing spot. The ship has facilities for undertaking 3 major operations simultaneously, intensive care, high dependency and general wards for up to 100 patients. It also has a dentistry operating theatre, CT scanner and X-ray units. The care facility operates with a staff of up to 250 doctors, nurses and support staff. The ship is scheduled to remain in service until 2020. In October 2014 she deployed off Sierra Leone in support of military and foreign aid personnel ashore who are fighting the Ebola outbreak. Her initial deployment was expected to last for six months.

MV Hurst Point

STRATEGIC SEALIFT RO-RO VESSELS
POINT CLASS

Ship	Pennant Number	Completion Date	Builder
HURST POINT	2002	Flensburger
HARTLAND POINT	2002	Harland & Wolff
EDDYSTONE	2002	Flensburger
ANVIL POINT	2003	Harland & Wolff

Displacement 10,000 tonnes, 13,300 tonnes (FL) **Dimensions** 193m x 26m x 6.6m
Speed 18 knots **Complement** 38

Notes

Foreland Shipping Limited operated 6 ro-ro vessels built at yards in the UK and Germany under a PFI deal which was signed with the MoD on 27 June 2002 and runs until 31 December 2024. While the current main focus is on transporting equipment to and from the Middle East/Gulf in support of military activities in Afghanistan, the vessels also make regular voyages to the Falkland Islands and to Canada and Norway in support of training exercises. The ships are all named after English lighthouses. The ships come under the operational umbrella of Defence Supply Chain Operation and Movements (DSCOM), part of the Defence Logistics Organisation. In 2012 the requirement was reduced from six to four ships. BEACHY HEAD and LONGSTONE were subsequently sold. The former has been renamed WILLIAMSBORG and is operated under the Maltese flag. The latter has been operating a Ro-Ro service in Australian waters between Burnie and Melbourne.

RFA BLACK ROVER with HMS IRON DUKE to starboard and FS COMMANDANT BLAISON to port

F234

A 273

F793

HMS DIAMOND

Michel Floch

Michael Nitz - Naval Press Service

HMS QUORN

M41

HMS SCIMITAR

Daniel Ferro

P284

RFA FORT ROSALIE

Andy Mahon

RFA WAVE KNIGHT

Daniel Ferro

SERCO MARINE SERVICES

In December 2007 the MoD signed a £1 billion Private Finance Initiative (PFI) contract with Serco Denholm Marine Services Limited for the future provision of marine services (FPMS) over the following 15 years. In 2009 Serco bought out Denholm's share and the SD funnel logos have been replaced by a prominent Serco logo on the superstructure.

Marine services embrace a wide range of waterborne and associated support activities, both in and out of port, at Portsmouth, Devonport and on the Clyde, as well as maintenance of UK and overseas moorings and navigational marks and support of a range of military operations and training.

In-port services include the provision of berthing and towage activities within the three naval bases; passenger transportation, including pilot transfers and the transportation of stores, including liquids and munitions. The recovery and disposal of waste from ships and spillage prevention and clean-up also fall within their tasking. There is also a requirement for substantial out-of-port operations. Diving training, minelaying exercises, torpedo recovery, boarding training and target towing duties are also undertaken.

The Briggs Group has been sub-contracted to assist with buoys and mooring support work. Shore based work to support these moorings and navigation buoys, have been relocated from Pembroke Dock to Burntisland on the Firth of Forth.

Initially all vessels were repainted with red funnels and black hulls, the white line having been removed as were, in most cases, the pennant numbers. All names are now prefixed with the letters 'SD' and all vessels fly the red ensign. In 2012, the last vestiges of the former RMAS identity were removed as, gradually, the whole fleet adopts a new colour scheme with the buff superstructure being repainted white.

SHIPS OF
SERCO MARINE SERVICES

Ship	Page	Ship	Page
SD ADEPT	70	SD MOORFOWL	88
SD BOUNTIFUL	69	SD MOORHEN	88
SD BOVISAND	79	SD NAVIGATOR	89
SD CAREFUL	70	SD NETLEY	80
SD CATHERINE	74	SD NEWHAVEN	80
SD CAWSAND	79	SD NORTHERN RIVER	87
SD CHRISTINA	72	SD NORTON	83
SD CLYDE RACER	90	SD NUTBOURNE	80
SD CLYDE SPIRIT	91	SD OBAN	82
SD DEBORAH	72	SD OCEANSPRAY	85
SD DEPENDABLE	69	SD OILMAN	85
SD EILEEN	72	SD OMAGH	82
SD EMILY	74	SD ORONSAY	82
SD ENGINEER	89	SD PADSTOW	81
SD EVA	84	SD POWERFUL	70
SD FAITHFUL	70	SD RAASAY	89
SD FLORENCE	73	SD RELIABLE	69
SD FORCEFUL	70	SD RESOURCEFUL	69
SD FRANCES	73	SD SOLENT RACER	90
SD GENEVIEVE	73	SD SOLENT SPIRIT	91
SD HELEN	73	SD SUZANNE	72
SD HERCULES	71	SD TAMAR RACER	90
SD IMPETUS	67	SD TAMAR SPIRIT	91
SD IMPULSE	67	SD TEESDALE	86
SD INDEPENDENT	68	SD TILLY	75
SD INDULGENT	68	SD VICTORIA	76
SD INSPECTOR	89	SD WARDEN	77
SD JUPITER	71	SD WATERPRESS	85
SD KYLE OF LOCHALSH	78		
SD MARS	71	**BRIGGS SUB-CONTRACT**	
SD MELTON	85		
SD MENAI	85	CAMERON	92
SD MEON	85	KINGDOM OF FIFE	92

SD Impetus

TUGS

IMPULSE CLASS

Ship	Completion Date	Builder
SD IMPULSE	1993	R. Dunston
SD IMPETUS	1993	R. Dunston

G.R.T. 400 tons approx **Dimensions** 33m x 10m x 4m **Speed** 12 knots **Complement** 5

Notes

Completed in 1993 specifically to serve as berthing tugs for the Trident Class submarines at Faslane. To be retained in service until 2022.

SD Independent

ASD 2509 CLASS

Ship	Completion Date	Builder
SD INDEPENDENT	2009	Damen, Gorinchem
SD INDULGENT	2009	Damen, Gorinchem

G.R.T. 345 tons approx **Dimensions** 26.09m x 9.44m x 4.3m **Speed** 13 knots **Complement** 5

Notes

Azimuth Stern Drive (ASD) tugs. Designed for Coastal and Harbour towage, specifically modified for making cold moves within the Naval Bases. Both are based at Portsmouth.

SD Bountiful

ATD 2909 CLASS

Ship	Completion Date	Builder
SD RELIABLE	2009	Damen, Stellendam
SD BOUNTIFUL	2010	Damen, Stellendam
SD RESOURCEFUL	2010	Damen, Stellendam
SD DEPENDABLE	2010	Damen, Stellendam

G.R.T. 271 tons **Dimensions** 29.14m x 9.98m x 4.8m **Speed** 13.1 knots **Complement** 5 (Accommodation for 6)

Notes

Azimuthing Tractor Drive (ATD) tugs. SD BOUNTIFUL is based at Portsmouth. SD RESOURCEFUL, SD RELIABLE and SD DEPENDABLE are based on the Clyde. Designed for Coastal and Harbour towage, specifically modified for making cold moves within the Naval Bases. Two double drum towing winches are fitted, along with extensive underwater fendering, fire fighting equipment and facilities for passenger and stores transportation.

SD Powerful

TWIN UNIT TRACTOR TUGS

Ship	Completion Date	Builder
SD ADEPT	1980	R. Dunston
SD CAREFUL	1982	R. Dunston
SD FAITHFUL	1985	R. Dunston
SD FORCEFUL	1985	R. Dunston
SD POWERFUL	1985	R. Dunston

G.R.T. 384 tons **Dimensions** 38.8m x 9.42m x 4m **Speed** 12 knots **Complement** 5

Notes

The principal harbour tugs in naval service. Some are to undergo a service life extension programme.

SD Hercules

STAN TUG 2608 CLASS

Ship	Completion Date	Builder
SD HERCULES	2009	Damen, Gorinchem
SD JUPITER	2009	Damen, Gorinchem
SD MARS	2009	Damen, Gorinchem

G.R.T. 133.92 tons **Dimensions** 26.61m x 8.44m x 4.05m **Speed** 12 knots **Complement** 4 (6 max)

Notes

A conventional Twin Screw Tug design. SD HERCULES and SD MARS are based at Devonport. SD JUPITER is based on the Clyde. All can be used to handle submarine mounted Towed Arrays.

SD Christina

ASD 2009 CLASS

Ship	Completion Date	Builder
SD CHRISTINA	2010	Damen, Gdynia
SD DEBORAH	2010	Damen, Gdynia
SD EILEEN	2010	Damen, Gdynia
SD SUZANNE	2010	Damen, Gdynia

G.R.T. 120.74 tons **Dimensions** 21.2m x 9.4m x 3.6m **Speed** 11 knots **Complement** 3/4

Notes

Azimuth Stern Drive tugs derived from the successful Damen ASD 2411 shiphandling tug. Winches fore and aft, together with a bow thruster, make these tugs suitable for handling smaller surface ship, barge work and assisting with submarine movements. SD DEBORAH and SD EILEEN are based at Devonport, SD CHRISTINA and SD SUZANNE at Portsmouth.

SD Genevieve

FELICITY CLASS

Ship	Completion Date	Builder
SD FLORENCE	1980	R. Dunston
SD FRANCES	1980	R. Dunston
SD GENEVIEVE	1980	R. Dunston
SD HELEN	1974	R. Dunston

G.R.T. 88.96 tons **Dimensions** 22.0m x 6.4m x 2.6m **Speed** 10 knots **Complement** 4

Notes

Water Tractors used for the movement of small barges and equipment. SD FRANCES and SD FLORENCE based at Devonport, with the other pair at Portsmouth.

73

SD Catherine

PUSHY CAT 1204

Ship	Completion Date	Builder
SD CATHERINE	2008	Damen, Gorinchem
SD EMILY	2008	Damen, Gorinchem

G.R.T. 29.4 tons **Dimensions** 12.3m x 4.13m x 1.55m **Speed** 8 knots **Complement** 2

Notes

Powered by a single Caterpillar 3056 TA diesel driving a single screw. A propulsion nozzle is fitted, and twin rudders to give a 2.1 tons bollard pull. SD CATHERINE is based at Portsmouth, SD EMILY at Devonport. General line runner and harbour workboat.

SD Tilly

STAN TUG 1405

Ship	Completion Date	Builder
SD TILLY	2009	Damen, Gorinchem

G.R.T. 45 tons **Dimensions** 14.55m x 4.98m x 1.8m **Speed** 9 knots **Complement** 3

Notes

A general purpose inshore and harbour tug based at Devonport. A twin screw version of the Pushy Cat 1204. Slightly larger with a bow thruster and also developing 8 tonnes bollard pull. Line handler, general workboat and ideal for moving small barges.

SD Victoria

WORLDWIDE SUPPORT VESSEL

Ship	Completion Date	Builder
SD VICTORIA	2010	Damen, Galatz

G.R.T. 3,522 tons **Dimensions** 83m x 16m x 4.5m **Speed** 14 knots **Complement** 16 (Accommodation for 72)

Notes

Powered by two Caterpillar 3516B diesels driving two shafts with controllable pitch propellers SD VICTORIA is designed to support training operations around the world. Capable of transporting both personnel and equipment and supporting diving operations. She is equipped with classrooms, briefing rooms and operations rooms in addition to workshop facilities. There is provision to carry and operate RIBs and there is a helicopter winching deck. Note Fast Interceptor Craft under covers on the quarterdeck.

SD Warden

TRIALS VESSEL

Ship	Completion Date	Builder
SD WARDEN	1989	Richards

Displacement 626 tons **Dimensions** 48m x 10m x 4m **Speed** 15 knots **Complement** 11

Notes

Built as a Range Maintenance Vessel but now based at Kyle of Lochalsh and operated in support of BUTEC. Also operates as a Remotely Operated Vehicle (ROV) platform. A replacement ROV has been installed and set to work to replace the older system. To remain in service until 2022.

SD Kyle of Lochalsh

TRIALS VESSEL

Ship	Completion Date	Builder
SD KYLE OF LOCHALSH	1997	Abel, Bristol

Displacement 120 tons **Dimensions** 24.35m x 9m x 3.45m **Speed** 10.5 knots **Complement** 4

Notes

The former twin screw tug MCS LENIE which has now been purchased from Maritime Craft Services (Clyde) Ltd by Serco Marine Services. The 24.35m tug, built in 1997 by Abel in Bristol, is powered by Caterpillar main engines producing a total of 2,200bhp for a bollard pull of 26 tons. She is used to support trials and operations at Kyle.

SD Cawsand

TENDERS
STORM CLASS

Ship	Completion Date	Builder
SD BOVISAND	1997	FBM (Cowes)
SD CAWSAND	1997	FBM (Cowes)

G.R.T 225 tonnes **Dimensions** 23m x 11m x 2m **Speed** 15 knots **Complement** 5

Notes

These craft are used in support of Flag Officer Sea Training (FOST) at Plymouth to transfer staff quickly and comfortably to and from Warships and Auxiliaries within and beyond the Plymouth breakwater in open sea conditions. These are the first vessels of a small waterplane area twin hull (SWATH) design to be ordered by the Ministry of Defence and cost £6.5 million each. Speed restrictions implemented due to wash problems generated by these vessels. To remain in service until 2022.

SD Nutbourne

NEWHAVEN CLASS

Ship	Completion Date	Builder
SD NEWHAVEN	2000	Aluminium SB
SD NUTBOURNE	2000	Aluminium SB
SD NETLEY	2001	Aluminium SB

Tonnage 77 tonnes (45 grt) **Dimensions** 18.3m x 6.8m x 1.88m **Speed** 10 knots
Complement 2/3 Crew (60 passengers)

Notes

MCA Class IV Passenger Vessels acquired as replacements for Fleet tenders. Employed on general passenger duties within the port area. To remain in service until 2022. SD NETLEY and NUTBOURNE are based at Portsmouth, SD NEWHAVEN at Devonport.

SD Padstow

PADSTOW CLASS

Ship	Completion Date	Builder
SD PADSTOW	2000	Aluminium SB

Tonnage 77 tonnes (45 grt) **Dimensions** 18.3m x 6.8m x 1.88m **Speed** 10 knots
Complement 2/3 Crew (60 passengers)

Notes

MCA Class IV, VI and VIA Passenger Vessel based at Devonport. Used on liberty runs
in Plymouth Sound and the Harbour as well as occasionally supporting FOST. To remain
in service until 2022.

81

SD Oransay

OBAN CLASS

Ship	Completion Date	Builder
SD OBAN	2000	McTay Marine
SD ORONSAY	2000	McTay Marine
SD OMAGH	2000	McTay Marine

G.R.T 199 tons **Dimensions** 27.7m x 7.30m x 3.75m **Speed** 10 knots **Complement** 4 Crew (60 passengers)

Notes

MCA Class IIA Passenger Vessels which replaced Fleet tenders in 2001. SD OBAN was transferred to Devonport in 2003 and is now primarily used to support FOST staff. SD ORONSAY and SD OMAGH employed on general passenger duties on the Clyde and are additionally classified as Cargo Ship VIII(A). To remain in service until 2022.

SD Norton

PERSONNEL FERRY

Ship	Completion Date	Builder
SD NORTON	1989	FBM Marine

G.R.T 21 tons **Dimensions** 15.8m x 5.5m x 1.5m **Speed** 13 knots **Complement** 2

Notes

The single FBM catamaran, 8837, operated at Portsmouth. Can carry 30 passengers or 2 tons of stores. Was a prototype catamaran designed to replace older Harbour Launches but no more were ordered.

SD Eva

PERSONNEL FERRY

Ship	Completion Date	Builder
SD EVA	2009	Damen

G.R.T 168 tons **Dimensions** 33.21m x 7.4m x 3.3m **Speed** 23.4 knots **Complement** 4-6 (plus 34 passengers)

Notes

Operated on the Clyde as a Fast Crew Transport. The Axe Bow design allows the vessel to effectively cut through waves with minimal movement of the vessel. The vessel is the first of its type in the UK to be operated under the International Code of Safety for High Speed Craft (HSC Code).

• BARRIE CLARK

SD Menai

FLEET TENDERS

Ship	Completion Date	Builder
SD MELTON	1981	Richard Dunston
SD MENAI	1981	Richard Dunston
SD MEON	1982	Richard Dunston

G.R.T. 117.3 tons **Dimensions** 24m x 6.7m x 3.05m **Speed** 10.5 knots **Complement** 4 (12 passengers)

Notes

The last three survivors of a once numerous class of vessels used as Training Tenders, Passenger Ferries, or Cargo Vessels. MENAI and MEON are operated at Falmouth. MELTON is operated at Kyle. A vessel replacement programme now seems unlikely and this elderly trio are expected to remain in service until 2022.

SD Teesdale

COASTAL OILER

Ship	Completion Date	Builder
SD TEESDALE	1976	Yorkshire Drydock Co.

G.R.T. 499 tons **Dimensions** 43.86m x 9.5m x 3.92m **Speed** 8 knots **Complement** 5

Notes

Formerly the oil products tanker TEESDALE H operated by John H Whitaker. Operates as a parcel tanker delivering diesel and aviation fuel and also delivering / receiving compensating water. She is self propelled by two Aquamaster thrusters.

A Diesel Lighter Barge, SD OILMAN, and a Water Lighter Barge, SD WATERPRESS, are operated on the Clyde. A further barge, a Liquid Mixed Lighter Barge, SD OCEANSPRAY, is based at Portsmouth.

SD Northern River

MULTI-PURPOSE VESSEL

Ship	Completion Date	Builder
SD NORTHERN RIVER	1998	Myklebust (Norway)

G.R.T 3,605 tons **Dimensions** 92.8m x 18.8m x 4.9m **Speed** 14 knots **Complement** 14

Notes

Bought from Deep Ocean AS (a subsidiary of Trico Marine) this Ulstein UT-745L designed Support Vessel entered service with Serco in March 2012. She can be employed on a variety of tasking from target towing, through noise ranging to data gathering; boarding training to submarine escort. Her extensive flat work deck allows her to embark containers for passive sonar training. She can also provide nuclear emergency support as well as support to submarine emergencies. She can provide mother ship training facilities for the NATO submarine Rescue System (NSRS), which involves the embarkation, fitting and operation of specialist ROV's, escape vessels and Transfer Under Pressure (TUP) facilities on the after deck, together with the embarkation of up to 40 additional personnel (see photo). She can also support the Submarine Parachute Assistance Group.

SD Moorhen

DIVING SUPPORT VESSELS
MOOR CLASS

Ship	Completion Date	Builder
SD MOORFOWL	1989	McTay Marine
SD MOORHEN	1989	McTay Marine

Displacement 518 tons **Dimensions** 32m x 11m x 2m **Speed** 8 knots **Complement** 10

Notes

Designed as a powered mooring lighter for use within sheltered coastal waters the lifting horns have been removed from the bows of both vessels when they were converted to Diving Support Vessels. They are used by the Defence Diving School for diving training in the Kyle of Lochalsh. To remain in service until 2022.

SD Navigator

MULTICAT 2510 CLASS

Ship	Completion Date	Builder
SD NAVIGATOR	2009	Damen, Hardinxveld
SD RAASAY	2010	Damen, Hardinxveld

G.R.T 150.27 tons **Dimensions** 26.3m x 10.64m x 2.55m **Speed** 8 knots **Complement** 3 (plus up to 12 additional personnel)

Notes

SD NAVIGATOR is equipped for buoy handling with a single 9 ton capacity crane. She is capable of supporting diving operations. SD RAASAY is based at the Kyle of Lochalsh. She is fitted with two cranes for torpedo recovery and support diving training. SD NAVIGATOR is managed from Portsmouth, but operates between Devonport and Portsmouth. Two similar vessels, SD INSPECTOR (ex-DMS EAGLE) and SD ENGINEER operate from Portsmouth and Devonport respectively.

SD Solent Racer

STAN TENDER 1505 CLASS

Ship	Completion Date	Builder
SD CLYDE RACER	2008	Damen, Gorinchem
SD SOLENT RACER	2008	Damen, Gorinchem
SD TAMAR RACER	2008	Damen, Gorinchem

Displacement 25.19 GRT **Dimensions** 16m x 4.85m x 1.25m **Speed** 20 knots **Complement** 3 (+ 10 Passengers)

Notes

Of aluminium construction these boats are employed on transfer of pilots, port security operations and passenger and VIP transportation.

SD Solent Spirit

STAN TENDER 1905 CLASS

Ship	Completion Date	Builder
SD CLYDE SPIRIT	2008	Damen, Gorinchem
SD SOLENT SPIRIT	2008	Damen, Gorinchem
SD TAMAR SPIRIT	2008	Damen, Gorinchem

Displacement 43.3 GRT **Dimensions** 18.91m x 5.06m x 1.65m **Speed** 21.7 knots **Complement** 3 (+ 10 passengers)

Notes

Steel hull with aluminium superstructure. Special propeller tunnels are fitted to increase propulsion efficiency and to reduce vibration and noise levels. These vessels are able to operate safely and keep good performance in wind speeds up to Force 6 and wave heights of 2 metres. Employed on transfer of pilots, VIPs and personnel.

Kingdom of Fife

ANCHOR HANDLING TUG

Ship	Completion Date	Builder
KINGDOM OF FIFE	2008	Damen, Galatz

Displacement 1,459 tons **Dimensions** 61.2m x 13.5m x 4.75m **Speed** 13.7 knots **Complement** 18

Notes

Briggs Marine won a £100m contract from Serco to support navigation buoy mainte-nance and mooring support for the Royal Navy for 15 years. During the contract peri-od, Briggs Marine provide support for over 350 moorings, navigation buoys and targets for the RN all around the UK coast, as well as Cyprus, Gibraltar and the Falkland Islands. KINGDOM OF FIFE was delivered in May 2008 and supports the existing Briggs Marine shallow draught and heavy lift craft CAMERON in servicing the contract, and is equipped with a decompression chamber and its own dedicated dive support team.

Smit Towy

AIRCREW TRAINING VESSELS

Ship	Comp Date	Builder	Base Port
SMIT DEE	2003	BES Rosyth	Buckie
SMIT DART	2003	BES Rosyth	Plymouth
SMIT DON	2003	BES Rosyth	Blyth
SMIT YARE	2003	FBMA Cebu	Great Yarmouth
SMIT TOWY	2003	FBMA Cebu	Pembroke Dock
SMIT SPEY	2003	FBMA Cebu	Plymouth

G.R.T. 95.86 GRT **Dimensions** 27.6m x 6.6m x 1.5m **Speed** 21 knots **Complement** 6

Notes

The service for Marine Support to Ranges and Aircrew Training is provided by SMIT (Scotland) Ltd and runs until April 2017. These vessels provide training for military aircrew in marine survival techniques, helicopter winching drills, target towing and general marine support tasks. More recently they have participated in Navy Command boarding exercises, simulating arms and drug smuggling activities and force protection exercises involving both Fast Attack Craft and Fast Inshore Attack Craft. SMIT DART completed as a passenger vessel with a larger superstructure. A smaller, second-hand vessel, SMIT TAMAR is employed in a similar role.

Smit Stour

RANGE SAFETY VESSELS

Ship	Comp Date	Builder
SMIT STOUR	2003	Maritime Partners Norway
SMIT ROTHER	2003	Maritime Partners Norway
SMIT ROMNEY	2003	Maritime Partners Norway
SMIT CERNE	2003	Maritime Partners Norway
SMIT FROME	2003	Maritime Partners Norway
SMIT MERRION	2003	Maritime Partners Norway
SMIT PENALLY	2003	Maritime Partners Norway
SMIT WEY	2003	Maritime Partners Norway
SMIT NEYLAND	2003	Maritime Partners Norway

G.R.T. 7.0 tons **Dimensions** 12.3m x 2.83m x 0.89m **Speed** 35 knots **Complement** 2

Notes

A class of 12 metre Fast Patrol Craft which operate on Range Safety Duties at Dover, Portland and Pembroke.

AWB Storm

ARMY VESSELS
WORK BOATS

Vessel	Pennant Number	Completion Date	Builder
STORM	WB41	2008	Warbreck Eng.
DIABLO	WB42	2008	Warbreck Eng.
MISTRAL	WB43	2008	Warbreck Eng.
SIROCCO	WB44	2008	Warbreck Eng.

Displacement 48 tonnes   **Dimensions** 14.75m x 4.30m **Speed** 10 knots
Complement 4

Notes

Part of the Army's strategic port operations in Southampton, but can be transported by a 'mother ship' to other ports and places like Iraq. Are often used as tugs for mexeflotes, positioning other pontoon equipment and for handling flexible pipelines. They have a fire-fighting capability. The Army also operate a number of smaller Combat Support Boats. Built by RTK Marine/VT Halmatic (now BAE) these are fast and rugged small craft, 8.8m long with a twin Hamilton waterjet propulsion system powered by twin 210hp diesel engines.

All Army RCL landing craft, listed in the previous edition, were withdrawn from service, without replacement, in May 2014.

BORDER FORCE
STAN PATROL 4207 CLASS

Vessel	Pennant Number	Completion Date	Builder
SEARCHER	-	2002	Damen
SEEKER	-	2001	Damen
VALIANT	-	2004	Damen
VIGILANT	-	2003	Damen

Displacement 238 GRT   **Dimensions** 42.8m x 7.11m x 2.52m   **Speed** 26+ knots **Complement** 12

Notes
Powered by two Caterpillar diesel engines these vessels are capable of reaching speeds above 26 knots. They are able to remain at sea for extended periods and in heavy weather conditions. They operate 24 hours a day, 365 days per year, through the employment of dual crews. There are ten crews for the five Border Force cutters comprising 120 seagoing staff, working two weeks on and two weeks off. Cutters are mostly deployed on a risk-led or intelligence-led basis detecting prohibited and restricted goods, boarding and searching ships and providing a law enforcement presence in remote and inaccesible areas. Vessels are prefixed HMC for Her Majesty's Cutter. The are recognised by a diagonal blue, white, red, white stripe on the bows.

96

HMC Protector

TELKKÄ CLASS

Vessel	Pennant Number	Completion Date	Builder
PROTECTOR	-	2002	UKI Workboat

Displacement 400 tonnes **Dimensions** 49.7m x 7.5m x 3.9m **Speed** 22 knots
Complement 12

Notes

In 2013 the Border Force purchased the former Finnish Border Agency vessel TAVI. Built by Uki Workboat Ltd, Uusikaupunki, Finland she is powered by 2 x Wärtsilä 12V200 Diesel Engines. She has replaced SENTINEL which was withdrawn from service in June 2013.

Babcock was awarded a contract by the Border Force in June 2011, to provide through-life maintenance and support for the force's fleet of five patrol boats. Under the contract each ship undergoes a docking period every two years and annual Life Saving Appliances (LSA) periods, taking one week, alongside. All five cutters are now based at Portsmouth.

AIRCRAFT OF THE FLEET AIR ARM

LOCKHEED MARTIN

Lockheed Martin LIGHTNING FRS1

Role Strike, fighter and reconnaissance aircraft
Engine 1 x Pratt & Whitney F135-PW-600 delivering 41,000lb thrust with reheat
Length 51' 4"   **Wingspan** 35'   **Height** 15'
Max Weight 60,000lb **Max Speed** Mach 1.6 **Crew** 1 pilot
Avionics AN/APG-81 AESA radar; AN/AAQ-40 electro-optical targeting system; AN/AAQ-37 distributed aperture system; AN/ASQ-239 'Barracuda' electronic warfare system; pilot's helmet-mounted display system; multi-function advanced data link.
Armament 2 internal weapons bays, each with separate hard points for a 1,000lb bomb equivalent and a single AIM-120 AMRAAM missile are used in 'stealth' mode. When stealth is not required, 7 external pylons can be fitted, 3 under each wing and one under the fuselage centreline allowing up to 12,000lb of fuel and weapons to be carried. Inner wing pylons can each carry a 426 US gallon drop tank. Block 3F software in operational British aircraft will allow the carriage of a wide range of US weapons plus the British ASRAAM air-to-air missile. A stockpile of US weapons is to be procured for British use.
Squadron Service 17 (Joint) Squadron, 617 (Joint) Squadron is due to form in 2016 to be followed by 809 (Joint) Squadron at a date which is yet to be announced.

Notes

British Lightning II units are operated by a mixture of RN and RAF personnel as joint units which will expand to form a Joint Lightning Force. 17 Squadron is based at Edwards AFB, California, as the UK element of the joint operational test team. UK pilots and maintenance personnel are trained by VMFAT-501 at MCAS Beaufort, South Carolina during 2015 as part of a UK/US agreement on carrier operations.

BAE Systems HAWK T 1

Role Role Operational training and threat simulation aircraft
Engine 1 x Rolls Royce Adour 151 delivering 5,200lb of thrust.
Length 40' 9" **Wingspan** 32' 7" **Height** 13' 1"
Max Weight 20,000lb **Max Speed** Mach 0.88 (Mach 1.2 in a dive) **Crew** 1 or 2 pilots
Avionics standard communications fit
Armament Can be fitted with a 30mm gun pod on a centreline pylon and one pylon
under each wing capable of taking AIM-9 Sidewinder or up to 1,500lb of practice
weapons

Squadron Service 736 Naval Air squadron

Notes

736 NAS acts as the focal point for fast jet experience within the RN command structure and provides pilots who have returned from flying USN fighters with continuation
experience in a UK environment. In due course, it will act as a lead-in training unit for
pilots destined to fly the Lightning. It also meets fleet requirements tasking including
the provision of aircraft for fighter controller and ASaC observer training and support
for FOST activities. It is based at RNAS Culdrose but maintains a detached flight at
RNAS Yeovilton.

AgustaWestland MERLIN HM2

Role Anti-submarine search and strike; maritime surveillance
Engines 3 x Rolls Royce/Turbomeca RTM 322 each developing 2,100 shp
Length 74' 10" **Rotor diameter** 61' **Height** 21' 10"
Max Weight 32,120lb **Max Speed** 167 knots **Crew** 1 or 2 pilots, 1 observer, 1 aircrewman
Avionics Blue Kestrel radar; Orange Reaper ESM; Folding Light Acoustic System for helicopters (FLASH); AQS-903 acoustic processor; Wescam MX-15 electro-optical/IR camera; defensive aids including Directional Infrared Countermeasures (DIRCM), AN/AAR-57 radar warning system, chaff and flare dispensers;
Armament Up to 4 Stingray torpedoes or Mark 11 depth charges; 1 x M3M 0.5" machine-gun in cabin door and 1 x 7.62mm machine-gun in cabin window

Squadron Service 814, 820, 824, 829 Naval Air Squadrons

Notes
30 Merlins have been upgraded to HM2 standard and are in service during 2015. 814 and 820 NAS embark in the Response Force Task Group LPH and RFAs; 829 NAS provides single aircraft flights to Type 23 frigates and 824 NAS is the type's training and operational development unit. All are shore based at RNAS Culdrose. Role-change radar and processing equipment is being identified for development under Project 'Crowsnest' that can be fitted to Merlin HM2s to allow them to operate in either the ASaC or anti-submarine roles when embarked in QUEEN ELIZABETH from 2018. 12 unconverted HM1s remain in storage with no planned future use at present.

100

AgustaWestland MERLIN HC3, HC3i and planned HC4

Role Commando assault, load-lifting, troop movement
Engines 3 x Rolls Royce/Turbomeca RTM 322 each developing 2,100 shp
Length 74' 10" **Rotor diameter** 61' **Height** 21' 10"
Max Weight 32,120lb **Max Speed** 167 knots **Crew** 1 or 2 pilots, 1 aircrewman
Avionics Wescam MX-15 electro-optical/IR camera; defensive aids suite including directional IR countermeasures, AN/AAR-57 missile approach warning system, automatic chaff and flare dispensers
Armament 1 x M3M 0.5" machine-gun in cabin door; 1 x 7.62mm machine-gun in cabin window

Squadron Service 846, 845 Naval Air Squadrons

Notes

The basic Merlin HC3 was operated by the RAF and lacks the ability to embark; 25 have now been handed over to the RN Commando helicopter Force as replacements for the Sea King HC4. 7 are modified to an interim HC3i standard capable of embarking with power-folding main rotor heads, lashing points and better communications. All 25 will eventually be upgraded to HC4 standard with, in addition to the interim fit, glass cockpits similar to the HM2 and power-folding tail pylons. 846 NAS reformed with HC3s in 2014 at RAF Benson and will move to RNAS Yeovilton in 2015. 845 will get its first HC 3s in mid 2015 and operate them alongside the remaining Sea King HC4s. Both units will be shore based at RNAS Yeovilton.

LEE HOWARD

AgustaWestland WILDCAT AH1, HMA2

Roles Surface search and strike; anti-submarine strike; boarding party support (HMA 2); reconnaissance and troop movement (AH 1)
Engines 2 x LHTEC CTS 800 each developing 1,362 shp
Length 50' **Rotor diameter** 42' **Height** 12'
Max Weight 13,200lb **Max Speed** 157 knots **Crew** 1 pilot & 1 observer
Avionics Selex-Galileo Sea Spray 7400E multi-mode AESA radar; Wescam MX-15 electro-optical/IR camera; Electronic warfare system and defensive aids suite. Bowman communications system
Armament 2 x Stingray torpedoes or Mark 11 depth charges; 1 x M3M 0.5" machine-gun in cabin door. To carry both heavy and light versions of future air-to-surface guided weapons from 2020.

Squadron Service 847, 825, 815 Naval Air Squadrons

Notes
The Wildcat has begun to replace the Lynx in operational service but delays in procuring the future air-to-service weapon will prevent it from reaching its full potential until 2020. 847 was the first unit to reach operational status with the AH1 in 2014 and operates as part of the Commando helicopter Force. Both 702 and 700W NAS were absorbed into a reformed 825 NAS in August 2014. The new unit will undertake Wildcat training and operational development and deploy the first 4 operational flights to sea. 815 will convert to the Wildcat HMA 2 from 2015 and take over the task of parenting flights from 825 NAS. All three NAS are shore-based at RNAS Yeovilton.

AgustaWestland LYNX HMA8

Roles Surface search and strike; anti-submarine strike; boarding party support
Engines 2 x Rolls Royce Gem BS 360-07-26 each developing 900 shp
Length 39' 1" **Rotor diameter** 42' **Height** 11'
Max Weight 9,500lb **Max Speed** 150 knots **Crew** 1 pilot & 1 observer
Avionics Sea Spray radar; Orange Crop ESM system; Sea Owl electro-optical/Infrared camera; STAURN communications system
Armament Up to 4 Sea Skua air-to-surface missiles or 2 Stingray torpedoes or 2 x Mark 11 depth charges. 1 x M3M 0.5" machine gun in cabin door and 1 hand-held Heckler & Koch G 3 sniper rifle to support boarding parties.

Squadron Service 815 Naval Air Squadron

Notes

Because of the delay in procuring surface-to-surface missiles for the Wildcat, a small number of Lynx are to be retained in service with 815 NAS, together with their Sea Skua missiles until March 2017. There will then be a gap in surface strike capability until 2020. 815 will begin to convert to the Wildcat in 2015 and take over the parenting of the first 4 flights from 825 NAS. It is shore-based at RNAS Yeovilton.

AgustaWestland SEA KING ASaC7

Role Airborne Surveillance and Control
Engines 2 x Rolls Royce Gnome H 1400 each developing 1,600 shp
Length 54' 9" **Rotor diameter** 62' **Height** 17' 2"
Max Weight 21,400lb **Max Speed** 125 knots **Crew** 1 pilot and 2 observers
Avionics Cerberus mission system; Searchwater radar; Orange Crop ESM; Link 16; AN/AAR-57 missile approach warning system; IR jammer; radar warning receiver; automatic chaff and flare dispenser
Armament none

Squadron Service 849, 854, 857 Naval Air Squadrons

Notes

7 Sea King ASaC7 are to be run on beyond their originally planned out-of-service date in 2016 until the third quarter of 2018 to fill the capability gap until 'Crowsnest' is developed. 854 and 857 NAS are expected to disband in late 2015 or early 2016 leaving 849 to provide training, operational development and the ability to embark in QUEEN ELIZABETH during her initial trials. The squadrons are shore-based at RNAS Culdrose.

LEE HOWARD

AgustaWestland SEA KING HC4

Role Commando assault; load-lifting and troop movement
Engines 2 x Rolls Royce Gnome H 1400 each developing 1,600 shp
Length 54' 9" **Rotor diameter** 62' **Height** 17' 2"
Max Weight 21,400lb **Max Speed** 125 knots **Crew** 1 pilot or 2 pilots, 1 aircrewman
Avionics AN/AAR-57 missile approach warning system; IR jammer; automatic chaff and flare dispenser
Armament 1 x M3M 0.5" machine-gun mounted in the cabin door and 1 x 7.62mm machine-gun in the crew entry door

Squadron Service 845 Naval Air Squadron

Notes

Most 'Jungly' Sea Kings have already been taken out of service but 11 Sea King HC 4 will be retained by 845 NAS until March 2016 to give a residual embarked capability to supplement the 7 Merlin HC 3i interim conversions. The Sea Kings will then be retired after 35 years in service leaving 845 NAS as a Merlin unit. It is shore-based at RNAS Yeovilton.

LEE HOWARD

AgustaWestland SEA KING HAR5

Roles Search and rescue; utility helicopter
Engines 2 x Rolls Royce Gnome H 14000 each developing 1,600 shp
Length 54' 9" **Rotor diameter** 62' **Height** 17' 2"
Max Weight 21,400lb **Max Speed** 125 knots **Crew** 2 pilots, 1 observer, 1 aircrewman
Avionics Sea Searcher radar; Sea Safire III electro-optical /camera
Armament None

Squadron Service 771 Naval Air squadron

Notes

771 NAS will provide SAR coverage throughout 2015 for the south-western UK from its base at RNAS Culdrose and will also operate a detachment of 3 aircraft at Prestwick which will cover a vast area of Scotland, Northern Ireland and out to 200 miles into the Atlantic. From 2016 civilian helicopters will take over the task under a Government contract, ending over 60 years of RN rescue operations in the UK. The Sea King HAR 5 will be withdrawn from service in March 2016 but no statement has been made about the future of 771 NAS.

Boeing SCANEAGLE

Role Unmanned surface search and reconnaissance
Engine 1 x Sonex heavy fuel (JP 5), pusher, piston engine developing 0.97KW
Length 5' 1" **Wingspan** 10' 3" **Height** 2'
Max Weight 48.5lb **Max Speed** 80 knots
Avionics EO900 electro-optical/IR imagers in a nose-mounted turret; analogue, digitally-encrypted control link; encrypted video downlink
Armament None

Notes

ScanEagle operating units are provided by Boeing under a 'contractor owned and operated' deal with the MoD although each detachment has an RN safety officer trained to 'fly' the air vehicle. They are deployed in selected frigates and RFAs in addition to manned helicopters to provide the parent ship's command team with real-time reconnaissance images out to 70 miles from the parent vehicle for up to 18 hours. The air vehicle is launched from a portable pneumatic catapult and is recovered by catching a vertical wire attached to the launcher unit with hooks on its wingtips. It is 'flown' throughout the mission by a pilot at a console in the parent ship's operations room. AgustaWestland has a contract in 2015 to evaluate future unmanned/optionally-manned helicopter concepts for the RN.

OTHER AIRCRAFT TYPES IN ROYAL NAVY SERVICE DURING 2015

CROWN COPYRIGHT/MoD 2011

Beech AVENGER T1

Role Observer training
Engines 2 x Pratt & Whitney PT6A-60A, each developing 1,050 shp
Length 46' 8" **Wingspan** 57' 11" **Height** 14' 4"
Max Weight 15,000lb **Max Speed** 313 knots
Crew 1 or 2 pilots, 4 student observers plus instructors
Avionics Surface search and ground mapping radar
Armament None

Squadron Service 750 Naval Air Squadron

Notes

750 NAS operates 4 Avengers as part of the Observer School at RNAS Culdrose to provide the third phase of the training syllabus. The first two phases are flown with 703 NAS at RAF Barkston Heath.

GROB TUTOR T1

Role Elementary training
Engine 1 x Textron Lycoming AE10-360-B1F developing 180 shp
Length 24' 9" **Wingspan** 32' 9" **Height** 7'
Max Weight 2,178lb **Max Speed** 185 knots **Crew** 2 pilots
Avionics None
Armament None

Squadron Service 703, 727 Naval Air Squadrons

Notes

703 NAS at RAF Barkston Heath provides elementary flying training for RN and RM pilots and the first two phases of RN observer training. 727 NAS at RNAS Yeovilton carries out the flying grading of newly entered RN and RM aircrew and other light fixed-wing tasks.

Eurocopter SQUIRREL HT1

Role Basic helicopter training
Engine 1 x Turbomeca Ariel 2D developing 847 shp
Length 35' **Rotor diameter** 36' **Height** 9' 3"
Max Weight 5,225lb **Max Speed** 155 knots **Crew** 2 pilots plus up to 5 passengers
Avionics None
Armament None

Squadron Service 705 Naval Air Squadron

Notes

705 NAS provides basic helicopter training for RN and RM pilots as part of the Defence Helicopter Flying School at RAF Shawbury.

Eurocopter AS365N DAUPHIN 2

Role Passenger movement and training support
Engines 2 x Turbomeca Arriel 2C each developing 838 shp
Length 39' 9" **Rotor diameter** 39' 2" **Height** 13' 4"
Max Weight 9,480lb **Max Speed** 155 knots **Crew** 1 or 2 pilots plus up to 11 passengers
Avionics None
Armament None

Notes

2 of these civil-owned, military registered helicopters are based at Newquay Airport and are used to support FOST activities in the Plymouth areas. Tasks include passenger transport and transfer between ships, radar calibration and spotting for naval gunfire support training. A new helicopter operating pad is to be built in Devonport Naval Base, due for completion in late 2015, from which FOST staff will be flown directly to and from ships at sea.

Royal Navy Historic Flight

Notes

Based at RNAS Yeovilton, the Flight includes Swordfish I W 5856; Swordfish II LS 326; Sea Fury FB 11 VR 930; Sea Fury T 20 VX 281; Sea Hawk WV 908 and Chipmunk T 10 WK 608. They are flown in displays by naval pilots and maintained by civilians under a MoD contract but are seldom all serviceable at the same time.

The Sea Fury T20 G-RNHF (VX 281) suffered engine failure during a display manoeuvre at RNAS Culdrose Air Day on 31 July 2014, forcing the pilot to make an emergency landing, during which the undercarriage collapsed. On 24 September 2014 it was transported from Culdrose to Weald Aviation Services, North Weald Airfield in Epping, Essex, for full assessment and repair.

In September 2014 the last airworthy Sea Vixen FAW 2, XP 924, was handed over to the Fly Navy Heritage Trust at RNAS Yeovilton. It will be operated alongside the aircraft of the RN Historic Flight.

ARMY AIR CORPS AND ROYAL AIR FORCE HELICOPTERS THAT CAN BE EMBARKED AS PART OF A TAILORED AIR GROUP

LEE HOWARD

AGUSTAWESTLAND APACHE AH 1

Notes Army Air Corps Apaches can be armed with up to 16 AGM-114 Hellfire missiles or up to 76 CRV-7 unguided rocket projectiles plus a single M230 30mm cannon with 1,160 rounds. Operated as part of the Joint Helicopter Force.

LEE HOWARD

BOEING CHINOOK

Notes RAF Chinooks are able to carry up to 44 fully equipped troops or a 20,000lb load and are armed with miniguns to give suppressive fire in assault landings. Operated as part of the Joint Helicopter Force.

WEAPONS OF THE ROYAL NAVY

Sea Launched Missiles

Trident II D5

The American built Lockheed Martin Trident 2 (D5) submarine launched strategic missiles are Britain's only nuclear weapons and form the UK contribution to the NATO strategic deterrent. 16 missiles, each capable of carrying up to 6 UK manufactured thermonuclear warheads (but currently limited to 4 under current government policy), can be carried aboard each of the Vanguard class SSBNs. Trident has a maximum range of 12,000 km and is powered by a three stage rocket motor. Launch weight is 60 tonnes, overall length and width are 13.4 metres and 2.1 metres respectively.

Tomahawk (BGM-109)

This is a land attack cruise missile with a range of 1600 km and can be launched from a variety of platforms including surface ships and submarines. Some 65 of the latter version were purchased from America to arm Trafalgar class SSNs with the first being delivered to the Royal Navy for trials during 1998. Tomahawk is fired in a disposal container from the submarine's conventional torpedo tubes and is then accelerated to its subsonic cruising speed by a booster rocket motor before a lightweight F-107 turbojet takes over for the cruise. Its extremely accurate guidance system means that small targets can be hit with precision at maximum range, as was dramatically illustrated in the Gulf War and Afghanistan. Total weight of the submarine version, including its launch capsule is 1816 kg, it carries a 450 kg warhead, length is 6.4 metres and wingspan (fully extended) 2.54 m. Fitted in Astute & T class submarines. It was announced in 2014 that the US Navy are to stop procuring the missile in 2015 which has implications for the production line. although an MoD spokesman expected this not to impact on UK requirements. In July 2014 the UK requested 65 missiles to replace those expended on coalition operations. In September 20 Block IV missiles were ordered.

Harpoon

The Harpoon is a sophisticated anti-ship missile using a combination of inertial guidance and active radar homing to attack targets out to a range of 130 km, cruising at Mach 0.9 and carrying a 227 kg warhead. It is powered by a lightweight turbojet but is accelerated at launch by a booster rocket. Fitted to Type 23 frigates, it is also the intention to refit four of the Type 45 destroyers with the systems removed from the decommissioned Batch III Type 22 frigates.

Sea Viper (Aster 15/30)

Two versions of the Aster missile will equip the Type 45 Destroyer, the shorter range Aster 15 and the longer range Aster 30. The missiles form the weapon component of the Principal Anti Air Missile System (PAAMS). Housed in a 48 cell Sylver Vertical Launch system, the missile mix can be loaded to match the ships requirement. Aster 15 has a range of 30 km while Aster 30 can achieve 100 km. The prime external difference between the two is the size of the booster rocket attached to the bottom of the missile. PAAMS is known as Sea Viper in RN service.

Sea Wolf

Short range rapid reaction anti-missile missile and anti-aircraft weapon. The complete weapon system, including radars and fire control computers, is entirely automatic in operation. Type 23 frigates carry 32 Vertical Launch Seawolf (VLS) in a silo on the foredeck. Basic missile data: weight 82 kg, length 1.9 m, wingspan 56 cm, range c.5-6 km, warhead 13.4 kg. The VLS missile is basically similar but has jettisonable tandem boost rocket motors.

Air Launched Missiles

Sea Skua

A small anti-ship missile developed by British Aerospace arming the Lynx helicopters carried by various frigates and destroyers. The missile weighs 147 kg, has a length of 2.85 m and a span of 62 cm. Powered by solid fuel booster and sustainer rocket motors, it has a range of over 15 km at high subsonic speed. Sea Skua is particularly effective against patrol vessels and fast attack craft, as was demonstrated in both the Falklands and Gulf Wars.

Guns

114mm Vickers Mk8 Mod 1

The Royal Navy's standard medium calibre general purpose gun which arms the Type 23 frigates and Type 45 destroyers. The Mod 1 is an electrically operated version of the original gun and is recognised by its angular turret. First introduced in 2001 it is now fitted in all Type 23 and Type 45 vessels. Rate of fire: 25 rounds/min. Range: 22,000 m. Weight of Shell: 21 kg.

Goalkeeper

A highly effective automatic Close in Weapons System (CIWS) designed to shoot down missiles and aircraft which have evaded the outer layers of a ships defences. The complete system, designed and built in Holland, is on an autonomous mounting and includes radars, fire control computers and a 7-barrel 30 mm Gatling gun firing 4200 rounds/min. Goalkeeper is designed to engage targets between 350 and 1500 metres away. However, with the decommissioning of the BIII Type 22 frigates and the carrier ILLUSTRIOUS there remains just the two mounts on the operational LPD. As a result the RN has determined to discontinue support for the system after 2015 and it is likely that during ALBIONs regeneration refit the system will be removed and replaced by either Phalanx or a more conventional close in systems. The same will happen to BULWARK when she enters refit in 2016.

Phalanx

A US built CIWS designed around the Vulcan 20 mm rotary cannon. Rate of fire is 3000 rounds/min and effective range is c.1500 m. Fitted in Type 45, OCEAN and some Wave, Bay and Fort classes. Block 1B began entering service from 2009. Incorporates side mounted Forward looking infra-red enabling CIWS to engage low aircraft and surface craft. In October 2012 it was announced that a further five Phalanx Block 1B mountings were to be procured to protect RFA ships

DS30B 30mm

Single mounting carrying an Oerlikon 30mm gun. Fitted to Type 23 frigates and various patrol vessels and MCMVs. In August 2005 it was announced that the DS30B fitted in Type 23 frigates was to be upgraded to DS30M Mk 2 to include new direct-drive digital servos and the replacement of the earlier Oerlikon KCB cannon with the ATK Mk 44 Bushmaster II 30 mm gun. Consideration is already being given to purchasing additional DS30M Mk 2 systems for minor war vessels and auxiliaries.

GAM BO 20mm

A simple hand operated mounting carrying a single Oerlikon KAA 200 automatic cannon firing 1000 rounds/min. Maximum range is 2000 m. Carried by most of the fleet's major warships except the Type 23 frigates.

20mm Mk.7A

The design of this simple but reliable weapon dates back to World War II but it still provides a useful increase in firepower, particularly for auxiliary vessels and RFAs. Rate of fire 500-800 rounds/min.

Close Range Weapons

In addition to the major weapons systems, all RN ships carry a variety of smaller calibre weapons to provide protection against emerging terrorist threats in port and on the high seas such as small fast suicide craft. In addition it is sometimes preferable, during policing or stop and search operations to have a smaller calibre weapon available. Depending upon the operational environment ships may be seen armed with varying numbers of pedestal mounted General Purpose Machine Guns (GPMG). Another addition to the close in weapons is the Mk 44 Mini Gun a total of 150 of which have been procured from the United States as a fleetwide fit. Fitted to a naval post mount, the Minigun is able to fire up to 3,000 rounds per minute, and is fully self-contained (operating off battery power).

Torpedoes

Stingray

A lightweight anti-submarine torpedo which can be launched from ships, helicopters or aircraft. In effect it is an undersea guided missile with a range of 11 km at 45 knots or 7.5 km at 60 knots. Length 2.1 m, diameter 330 mm. Type 23s have the Magazine Torpedo Launch System (MTLS) with internal launch tubes. Sting Ray Mod 1 is intended to prosecute the same threats as the original Sting Ray but with an enhanced capability against small conventionally powered submarines and an improved shallow-water performance.

Spearfish

Spearfish is a submarine-launched heavyweight torpedo which has replaced Tigerfish. Claimed by the manufacturers to be the world's fastest torpedo, capable of over 70 kts, its sophisticated guidance system includes an onboard acoustic processing suite and tactical computer backed up by a command and control wire link to the parent submarine. Over 20ft in length and weighing nearly two tons, Spearfish is fired from the standard 21-inch submarine torpedo tube and utilises an advanced bi-propellant gas turbine engine for higher performance.

Future Weapons

Sea Venom

Formerly known as the Future Anti-Surface Guided Weapon (Heavy), Sea Venom is high-sub-sonic 'drop-launch' missile in the 110 kg-class incorporating an imaging infrared seeker (with provisions for an additional semi-active laser guidance channel), a two-way datalink for oper-ator-in-the-loop control, and a 30kg warhead. Designed by MBDA to replace the helicopter air-launched Exocet, the missile will have a range of up to 25 km and will be able to counter targets up to corvette size. The FASGW programme, comprising both Heavy and Light mis-siles, is a joint venture between the UK and France. The missile will equip the RNs Wildcat helicopter and, in July 2014, AgustaWestland received a £90 million contract to integrate the respective variants for deployment from the Wildcat HMA2. Each aircraft will be able to carry four missiles and it is anticipated that Initial Operating Capability will be achieved in 2020, although there are aspirations that this date will move left.

Martlet

Formerly known as the Future Anti-Surface Guided Weapon (Light), this missile is designed to counter small boat and fast inshore attack craft threats. It is based on the laser beam-riding variant of the Thales Lightweight Multi-role Missile (LMM). With a range of up to 8 km it car-ries a 3 kg blast fragmentation/shaped charge warhead travelling at about Mach 1.5. Missiles will be carried in a five-round launcher (with each Wildcat able to carry up to four launchers). Alternatively a mix of two Sea Venom on the outer pylon and two five round Martlet on the inner weapons station can be carried. An active laser guidance unit integrated within the L-3 Wescam nose turret will support laser beam-riding guidance. Trials of both variants of FASGW are planned to take place between late 2018 to late 2019.

Sea Ceptor

Incorporating the Common Anti-Air Modular Missile (CAAMM) family, being developed to replace the Rapier and Seawolf SAM systems, plus the ASRAAM short range Air-to-Air Missile. It will arm the Royal Navy's Type 23 frigates and its Type 26 Global Combat Ships. In Spring 2012 the MoD awarded MBDA UK a five-year Demonstration Phase contract worth £483 million to develop the missile for the RN. In September 2013 a £250 million contract was announced to manufacture the missile in the UK, sustaining around 250 jobs at MBDA sites in Stevenage, Filton and Lostock. Installation of the Sea Ceptor on Type 23 frigates is due to start in 2015 and be completed by 2021.

At the end of the line ...

Readers may well find other warships afloat which are not mentioned in this book. The majority have fulfilled a long and useful life and are now relegated to non-seagoing duties. The following list gives details of their current duties:

Pennant No	Ship	Remarks
	BRITANNIA	Ex Royal Yacht at Leith. Open to the public.
	CAROLINE	Light Cruiser and veteran of the Battle of Jutland. Is to be restored and opened as a tourist attraction at Belfast.
	M33	Coastal Monitor. To be brought back to life at Portsmouth in time for 2015 Gallipoli Campaign commemorations following £1.79m lottery funding. Ownership to transfer to National Museum of the Royal Navy.
M29	BRECON	Hunt Class Minehunter - Attached to the New Entry Training Establishment, HMS RALEIGH, Torpoint, as a static Seamanship Training Ship.
M103	CROMER	Single Role Minehunter - Attached to BRNC, Dartmouth as a Static Training Ship.
L3505	SIR TRISTRAM	Refitted as a Static Range Vessel at Portland.
C35	BELFAST	World War II Cruiser Museum ship - Pool of London. Open to the public daily. Tel: 020 7940 6300
D23	BRISTOL	Type 82 Destroyer - Sea Cadet Training Ship at Portsmouth.
D73 S17	CAVALIER OCELOT	World War II Destroyer & Oberon class Submarine Museum Ships at Chatham. Open to the public. Tel: 01634 823800
M1115	BRONINGTON	The ship remains at Birkenhead, in poor condition, whilst discussions over its future continue.
S67	ALLIANCE	Submarine - Museum Ship at Gosport Open to the public daily. Tel: 023 92 511349
S50	COURAGEOUS	Nuclear-powered Submarine - On display at Devonport Naval Base. Can be visited during Base Tours. Tel: 01752 552326 for details.
M1151	IVESTON	Sold to private owner 2014 (Tilbury)
LCT7074	LANDFALL	A D-Day veteran. Refloated in October 2014 six years after she sank at Birkenhead. To be restored by the NMRN at Portsmouth following a £916,000 grant.

At the time of publishing (December 2014) the following ships were laid up in long term storage or awaiting sale.

PORTSMOUTH: Illustrious; Gloucester; York; Edinburgh; Walney.

PLYMOUTH: Tireless; Trafalgar; Turbulent; Sceptre; Superb; Splendid; Spartan; Sovereign; Conqueror; Valiant; Warspite.

ROSYTH: Resolution; Renown; Repulse; Revenge; Swiftsure; Churchill; Dreadnought.

Since the previous edition the following vessels in long term storage or awaiting scrap were disposed of:

LIVERPOOL: Departed Portsmouth under tow of tug PANTODYNAMOS on 22 October 2014 bound for recycling at Leyal Shipbreakers, Turkey.

MANCHESTER: Departed Portsmouth under tow of tug HELLAS on 14 November 2014 bound for recycling at Leyal Shipbreakers, Turkey.

PLYMOUTH: Departed Birkenhead under tow of tug AMBER II on 22 October 2014 bound for recycling in Turkey.

ONYX: Departed Barrow-in -Furness on 1 May 2014 bound for Rosneath on the Clyde, where she arrived the following day under tow of the tug BRUISER. Recycling commenced in July.